Justice, Jesus, and the Jews

A Proposal for Jewish-Christian Relations

Michael L. Cook, S.J.

M G

A Michael Glazier Book

THE LITURGICAL PRESS
Collegeville, Minnesota

www.litpress.org

A Michael Glazier Book published by The Liturgical Press.

Cover design by David Manahan, O.S.B. Illustration courtesy of Flat Earth Photos: Middle East.

Unless otherwise noted, all translations from the Bible are from Bruce M. Metzger and Roland E. Murphy, eds., *The New Oxford Annotated Bible* [NRSV] (New York: Oxford University Press, 1991). This includes chapter and verse numbering where they differ from the Masoretic text [MT]. The Hebrew Masoretic text employed is the New Jewish Publication Society Edition [NJPS], *JPS Hebrew-English Tanakh,* 2d ed. (Philadelphia: The Jewish Publication Society, 1999); first edition published in 1985. The transliteration of the Hebrew and Greek text follows the system employed in Raymond E. Brown, Joseph A. Fitzmyer, Roland E. Murphy, eds., *The New Jerome Biblical Commentary* (Englewood Cliffs, N.J.: Prentice-Hall, 1990) xlvi.

1 2 3 4 5 6 7 8

Library of Congress Cataloging-in-Publication Data

Cook, Michael L. (Michael LaVelle), 1936–
Justice, Jesus, and the Jews : a proposal for Jewish-Christian relations / Michael L. Cook.
p. cm.
"A Michael Glazier book."
Includes bibliographical references (p.) and index.
ISBN 0-8146-5148-8 (alk. paper)
1. Jesus Christ—Jewishness. 2. Christianity and other religions—Judaism. 3. Judaism—Relations—Christianity. 4. Justice. I. Title.

BT590.J8 C66 2003
261.2'6—dc21 2002075423

For John H. Wright, S.J.
Teacher
Scholar
Mentor
Colleague
Friend in the Lord
And for All of My Former Teachers
Ad Multos Annos

Contents

Acknowledgments

Books are not written without a wide range of support and encouragement. I am grateful to all but can mention only a few here. First, I wish to acknowledge Gonzaga University for granting me a sabbatical in 2000–2001, and especially the Jesuit Institute at Boston College for granting me a fellowship that enabled me to spend the year there in research and writing. I am particularly indebted to the director of the Jesuit Institute, Michael J. Buckley, S.J., and to his support staff for providing an agreeable and helpful environment in which to work. In that connection, I also thank the Jewish-Christian Seminar for inviting me to participate in their ongoing discussions. Professor Ruth Langer of the theology department and a member of the seminar read early portions of the manuscript and offered helpful comments. I am also grateful to Richard J. Clifford, S.J., of Weston Jesuit School of Theology and to Frederick L. Moriarty, S.J., of Boston College, both of whom read an early draft of the first two chapters and offered very helpful comments on the notion of justice in the Hebrew Bible. Likewise, I must thank my colleague at Gonzaga, Robert A. Kugler, who read the entire manuscript and engaged me in lively conversation about the issues involved. In this connection I also thank all of my colleagues in the religious studies department at Gonzaga for their unfailing support. I am most deeply grateful to Boston College not only for providing an excellent working environment, including its very fine library, but also for providing a very welcoming and agreeable living environment in the Jesuit Community. I am especially grateful to the rector, Francis R. Herrmann, S.J., and to the denizens of Roberts House where I lived and enjoyed many lively conversations. Finally, I must mention Nancy Masingale, director of faculty services at Gonzaga, for her indispensable help in the land of computers, and Annette Kmitch, editor at The Liturgical Press, for her competence in the editing process. This book is dedicated to John H. Wright, S.J., and to all my former teachers, without whom a book like this could never have been conceived.

Introduction

On September 10, 2000, "an interdenominational group of Jewish scholars" published in the *New York Times* a Jewish statement on Christians and Christianity entitled *Dabru Emet,* citing Zechariah 8:16: "These are the things you are to do: Speak the truth to one another, render true and perfect justice in your gates."[1] The statement notes that since the Holocaust "Christianity has changed dramatically" and that many official Church bodies have published statements of "remorse about Christian mistreatment of Jews and Judaism" and of the need to reform Christian teaching and preaching "so that they acknowledge God's enduring covenant with the Jewish people and celebrate the contribution of Judaism to world civilization and to Christianity itself." Such changes "merit a thoughtful Jewish response," and so eight brief statements are offered on "how Jews and Christians can relate to each other."[2] Although all the issues mentioned are important and will come into play in the present work, the last will receive particular focus: "Jews and Christians must work together for justice and peace. . . . Although justice and peace are finally God's, our joint efforts, together with those of other faith communities, will help bring the kingdom of God for which we hope and long."

Justice, and the peace which is its fruit (Isa 32:17), is an issue that can unite Jews and Christians rather than divide them. Yet, while we can rally around contemporary concerns such as poverty and human degradation in the present "unredeemed state of the world," this book proposes to explore the foundational question of how justice is to be understood as mediated through the written Torah of the Hebrew tradition and the oral proclamation of the historical Jesus. In particular, was Jesus seeking to evoke and express what was deepest and best in the traditions of his own people? The proposal is to move back to a stage of history prior to the so-called "parting of the ways"[3] and to ask whether the aim of Jesus was to bring justice to his own people and in what sense; i.e., does his proclamation of God's reign (or kingdom) correspond to the deepest yearning of the people Israel: "I will bring them to live in Jerusalem. They shall be my people and I will be their God, in faithfulness and in righteousness" (Zech 8:8; cp. Exod 6:6-8; Jer 31:33)? The purpose of this work is not to obviate the clear difference between Judaism and Christianity as religions in their own right, with their distinctive traditions and histories. Quite the contrary, the purpose is to affirm the validity of each tradition in its faithfulness to its own revelation. I concur with the sixth statement of *Dabru Emet:* "The humanly irreconcilable difference between Jews and Christians will not be settled until God redeems the entire world as promised in Scripture." Profound differences do exist and any final unification and reconciliation awaits God's future.[4] However, while the differences remain and must be respected, there are many issues that bring us together, as witnessed in the statement *Dabru Emet*. Not the least of these is justice.

The retrieval of the Hebrew notion of justice and Jesus' relationship to it may serve to challenge and to renew both the Jewish and the Christian traditions and to provide a lens for developing a closer relationship in these more ecumenical times. Such, at least, is the hope and project of this book. But there are difficulties along the way and distinctions that must be made. Chapter 1 will review some current issues in Jewish-Christian relations, specifically whether Jewish-Christian dialogue is possible, the necessity and difficulty in reading each other's texts (using the Gospel of Matthew as an example), three ways in which the Hebrew Scriptures are read, and finally the key issue of this book as it emerges in relation to other possible issues. Chapter 2 will then elicit from a reading of the Tanakh (the Hebrew canon of the written Torah that includes the Pentateuch *[Torah]*, the Prophets *[Neviʾim]*, and the Writings *[Kethuvim]*) a biblical, rather than "liberal" or other contemporary, understanding of justice. Corresponding to the Hebrew understanding of justice, Chapter 3 will employ the methods of historical criticism as applied to the Gospels in order to engage the question of what Jesus might have intended by justice in his historical mission to Israel. The idea is to demonstrate a point by point correlation between a coherent and self-contained vision of justice as found in the Hebrew Bible and Jesus' proclamation of God's reign. This will give us a new or different optic to view the relationship between Judaism and Christianity as two religions that have developed their own separate and distinct ways, especially from the fifth century on.

In metaphorical terms, does Jesus in his historical mission form a "bridge" across which both Jews and Christians can walk to greet one another? The Gospel of John sees Jesus as the "ladder" between heaven and earth envisioned by Jacob (John 1:51; Gen 28:12). The blessing of Jacob, the blessing of land and offspring, extends to "all the families of the earth" (Gen 28:13-15) but has to be won by struggling with both God and humans and prevailing (Gen 32:24-30). Behind John's appropriation of the symbols of Israel, can we still perceive the historical reality of Jesus the Jew whose life and mission were dedicated to that very blessing promised to Jacob-Israel?[5] This is a question that penetrates not only into the hopes and longings of the people Israel at the time of Jesus but also into the very essence of what we mean by Christian faith. It has always been so. For Jews can live without Christian faith, but Christians cannot live without the Jewish Jesus. And when they have tried to deny his Jewishness, they have distorted the nature of that faith.

Notes

[1] The *New York Times,* Sunday, September 10, 2000, p. 23. Just five days earlier, on September 5, the Congregation for the Doctrine of Faith under the signature of Joseph Cardinal Ratzinger published the declaration "'*Dominus Jesus'*: On the Unicity and Salvific Universality of Jesus Christ and the Church" (dated August 6, 2000). A phrase cited from John Paul II's encyclical *Redemptoris Missio* to the effect that interreligious dialogue is "part of the Church's evangelizing mission" has raised serious questions about the intention of the Vatican; namely, does this imply that the purpose of dialogue is conversion and baptism, something totally alien to the Jewish understanding of dialogue? A more nuanced statement that can be interpreted in the sense of openness to the truth and convictions of the partner in dialogue is from Joseph Cardinal Ratzinger (*Many Religions—One Covenant: Israel, the Church and the World,* trans. Graham Harrison [San Francisco: Ignatius Press, 1999] 112): ". . . proclamation of the gospel must be necessarily a dialogical process."

[2] Soon after a book was published that includes the original statement and a collection of essays mostly by Jewish scholars with responses from Christian scholars. Tikva Frymer-Kensky, David Novak, Peter Ochs, David Fox Sandmel, Michael A. Signer, eds., *Christianity in Jewish Terms* (Boulder, Colo.: Westview Press, 2000).

[3] James D. G. Dunn, ed., *Jews and Christians: The Parting of the Ways:* A.D. *70 to 135* (Grand Rapids, Mich.: Eerdmans Publishing, 1999; orig. 1992).

[4] Ratzinger, *Many Religions,* 109, comments: "Let me speak plainly: Anyone who expects the dialogue between religions to result in their unification is bound for disappointment. This is hardly possible within our historical time, and perhaps it is not even desirable."

[5] The Gospel of John is often characterized either as being itself anti-Jewish or as being a powerful source and inspiration for the horrendous history of anti-Semitism. While the second is true insofar as John has been misused, the first needs qualification. While it is true that John engages in a heated polemic with his Jewish contemporaries, a case could be made that John, paradoxically enough, is the most Jewish of the four Gospels. Matthew, especially in his engagement with and interpretation of Torah, is "thoroughly Jewish." Anthony J. Saldarini, in his very fine book *Matthew's Christian-Jewish Community* (Chicago: University of Chicago Press, 1994), has made this point extremely well. John, however, evokes in an even more striking way than Matthew the powerful images and symbols that constitute the very identity of Israel—such as the *shekinah,* the lamb of God, Jacob's ladder, the marriage feast, the Temple, the manna in the desert, the various festivals with their symbols of water and light, and so on. Jacob Neusner, while preferring "Matthew's Jesus" because "there really is a shared Torah," dismisses John's Jesus far too easily: "I cannot conceive an argument with John's Jesus, because eternal Israel in John is treated with unconcealed hatred" (Jacob Neusner, *A Rabbi Talks with Jesus* [Montreal/Ithaca, N.Y.: McGill-Queen's University Press, 2000; revised & expanded from 1993] 28 [cf. also 7–9]). Yet Neusner affirms in response to E. P. Sanders' notion of "covenantal nomism" that identity as the people Israel is more fundamental to the covenant than observance of the Law: "the covenant matters because of Israel and endures in Israel, even in its sinners." Jacob Neusner, *Telling Tales: Making Sense of Christian and Judaic Nonsense: The Urgency and Basis for Judeo-Christian Dialogue* (Louisville: Westminster/John Knox Press, 1993) 92, n. 14. If John had such "unconcealed hatred" for "eternal Israel," why would he even bother to employ her most powerful symbols and images? Is the author not engaging the very question of Israel's identity? For a nuanced and balanced view of "anti-Judaism in the Gospels," see George M. Smiga, *Pain and Polemic: Anti-Judaism in the Gospels* (Mahwah, N.J.: Paulist Press, 1992). Also, for an enlightening "ethical" reading of John that explores four approaches, namely a "compliant reading," "a resistant reading," "a sympathetic reading," and "an engaged reading," see Adele Reinhartz, *Befriending the Beloved Disciple: A Jewish Reading of the Gospel of John* (New York: Continuum, 2001).

CHAPTER ONE

"Speak the Truth to One Another" (Zech 8:16)

Issues in Jewish-Christian Relations

In a recent book Mary Boys speaks of a new vision of Jews and Christians as partners: "Each exists in her own integrity and vitality. Both are recipients of God's blessing, both true ways to God. They are partners in witnessing to and working for the reign of God."[1] There is, however, a gap between the official statements of Church bodies referred to in *Dabru Emet* and the awareness of such changes among Christians as a whole: "Christians as a whole, however, seem unaware of the dramatic changes implied in the pronouncements of modern church leaders. To put it bluntly, Jewish-Christian dialogue is peripheral in the church. *Too few Christians seem to realize that this dialogue is at heart a matter of justice.*"[2] This justice means, among other possibilities, that Christians must take Judaism seriously as a source of Christian self-understanding (which is the subtitle of the book), i.e., that the process of religious education among Christians must replace the "conventional account of Christian origins" with "an alternative account" that no longer teaches that Christians have replaced Jews as God's people (supersessionism).[3]

Writing twenty years after the first publication of his book, Edward Flannery decries the fact that the first objective of the original publication (in 1965), "to acquaint Christians generally with the immense sufferings of the Jews throughout the Christian era," has not been realized. In discussing the roots of anti-Semitism at the end, he concludes that education and dialogue are not enough.

> Antisemitism resides in the heart as much, if not more than, in the head. Education is essential, but more so is a change of heart, that *metanoia* which opens the mind to truth and moves the will to righteous action. More than a problem of education, antisemitism is a matter of conscience.[4]

In reviewing Church teaching across the Christian denominations toward the end of her book, Boys sees a "new posture" around six themes. The first three reveal a strong consensus among the Christian Churches: refutation of the charge of deicide, repudiation of anti-Semitism, and repentance in the wake of the Shoah (Holocaust). The other three are more controversial with varying degrees of assent: the rejection of the proselytizing of Jews which touches the nature of Christian mission, the review of teaching about Jews and Judaism which touches the theory and practice of Christian education, and the recognition of the state of Israel which touches the core of Jewish self-identity.[5] While recognizing the value of posing the issues in this way, there remains an underlying issue that challenges both Jewish and Christian identity, the nature of dialogue itself, and its implications for the way we read the Scriptures. As a matter of justice, this too is a matter of conscience.

Is Jewish-Christian Dialogue Possible?

Jacob Neusner maintains that "there has never been a Judeo-Christian dialogue"—though he wishes to show how we are now ready for one, at least among Jews and Christians in the United States, Britain, and France—because "neither side has tried to make sense of the other in the other's terms."[6] What then are the conditions that would make such a dialogue possible? There are at least four such conditions that one can elicit from Neusner's discussion. His views correspond closely with some of the observations of Cardinal Ratzinger.

The first and foundational condition is clear: "For dialogue to commence, there must be a community of shared experience." Neusner affirms this in reference to the current historical situation, but it entails "intellectual vitality" and "enlightened respect" that enables the dialogue partner both to think about the other in one's own terms and to articulate that thought in terms the other can grasp.[7] This is an invitation to enter into a conversation that will be intelligible to both partners and that assumes a prior recognition, or repentance (a "turning around" in the sense of the Hebrew word *shuv*), of both "the Christian invention of 'Judaism'" and "the Judaic dismissal of Christianity." There has been no dialogue because each has invented the other and formulated imaginary arguments in the manner of a monologue that is both disingenuous and false. On this point, Cardinal Ratzinger would concur: "False simplifications only do damage to the dialogue with the religions and to the dialogue with the Jewish faith." And further: "Jews and Christians should accept each other in profound inner reconciliation, neither in disregard of their faith nor in denying it, but out of the depth of faith itself."[8]

The second condition flows from the first: the need for clarity about the issues. For both authors this means a strong affirmation of the traditional understanding of the respective faith: for orthodox Christians, the unity of the Old and New Testaments and the high Christology of the Gospels and the councils; for rabbinic Jews, the eternal covenant with Israel and the revelation of both written (Tanakh) and oral (Talmud) Torah to Moses on Mount Sinai. Neither author has much use for questions about the historical Jesus. Ratzinger is highly critical of the "historico-critical method" on two counts. It calls into question the Christian interpretation of the Old Testament: "For if the Old Testament does not speak of Christ, it is not a Bible for Christians." And it relativizes Christology in the New Testament: "If Christ were only a misunderstood Jewish rabbi or a political rebel executed by the Romans for political reasons, what significance would his message have now?"[9]

Similarly, Neusner, in a section highly critical of Samuel Sandmel's approach in *We Jews and Jesus,* refers to this "trivializing Judaic Christology" as "monumentally irrelevant to authentic dialogue between faithful Christians and practicing Jews." He points to Sandmel's own admission of the inability to understand the Christian use of such terms as sin, atonement, and salvation as "the critical dilemma of dialogue" that renders the historical Jesus "simply inconsequential" in the dialogue. "Either Judaism addresses Jesus Christ God Incarnate or it fails to address Christianity at all."[10]

Since this perspective strikes at the very center of what is being proposed in the present work, some preliminary comments are in order while reserving a fuller discussion for later. If one wishes to limit the conversation to a fully developed rabbinic Judaism vis-à-vis a fully developed orthodox Christianity, as Neusner and Ratzinger do, then it does seem necessary to set up the terms of the dialogue, as Neusner does, by moving it away from doctrinal considerations toward "a different kind of dialogue" based on sympathetic imagination. If the Mishnah can say of Torah: "Turn it and turn it again, for everything is contained therein,"[11] the Christian tradition can say the same of the death and resurrection of Jesus. Everything that Christian faith says about him is "contained therein." This will not change and is not at issue here, though both Torah and Christ are open to "eternal interpretability." But an authentic dialogue that would invoke sympathetic imagination cannot simply ignore the essential and necessary distinction between Christianity as a religion born out of the experience of Jesus' death and resurrection, which then developed its self-understanding over many centuries, and Jesus in his historical mission who, as integral to that self-understanding, may well have something to say to the Christian tradition as well as to the Rabbinic tradition. It is simply not true to say that the historical Jesus is irrelevant and inconsequential to "faithful Christians" as distinct from the scholarly few. From personal experience over the years, using historical Jesus material in homilies and public talks on a popular level, I have found that the average "person-in-the-pew" is not only interested but fascinated by what can be said historically of Jesus. This phenomenon is also amply attested by the plethora of popular books and magazine articles, as well as other media like films and shows on television, that raise directly questions about the historical Jesus. If relevant to so many "faithful Christians," then also to the dialogue between Christians and Jews, for the concreteness and specificity of the historical Jesus in all his Jewishness touches the very essence of Christian faith. With this in mind, it is still true to say that dialogue in seeking clarity about the issues includes the need to understand each other's terms and to speak to the same issue. In *A Rabbi Talks with Jesus,* Neusner identifies the latter as "a shared Torah." This is a valid issue for dialogue, but we will discuss it not in reference to "Matthew's Jesus" but in reference to the historical Jesus and his proclamation of God's reign of justice.

The third condition for dialogue is stated as Neusner moves from doctrine to imagination, his "different kind of dialogue": "Dialogue will begin with the recognition of difference, with a search for grounds for some form of communication, rather than with the assumption of sameness and the search for commonalities."[12] His "new foundation for dialogue" means that one must understand the other within one's own terms, i.e., within the resources of one's own tradition. This includes, of course, the readiness to affirm the right to exist and the personal integrity of the other, and above all to let each one define himself or herself—principally in the stories they tell. Each must respect and seek to make sense of the "most deeply held convictions" of the other, as Neusner sees it: God incarnate for Christians and the uniqueness and holiness of Israel for Jews. To do this, we must move from the attempt to resolve theological or doctrinal disputes to an imaginative and sympathetic understanding of the other. Neusner asks: "To begin with, can I sympathize: that is, feel how the other feels, the other remaining other? The answer is, Yes, I can, if I find in my own world analogies that permit me in some measure to feel and so understand what the other feels and affirms in the world of that other."[13]

The question as to what we can identify with in the religious experience of the other calls for two comments in the light of Neusner's proposal of a new foundation for dialogue. First, one is reminded of the conclusion to William James's extensive survey of the varieties of religious experience, namely that religions tend to converge around ethical concerns and mystical/contemplative experiences and they tend to diverge when it comes to teachings or doctrinal disputes.[14] Neusner's move from theological or doctrinal differences to sympathetic feeling seems to confirm this. When he proposes "a Judaic telling of the Christian tale," he asks: "Can we find in the resources of Judaism a way of understanding what Christians might mean when they speak of Jesus Christ God Incarnate?" Yet the appeal is more to a mystical/contemplative kind of experience via Abraham Heschel's notion of God's personal self-involvement in human experience so that the prophets feel the very feelings of God. When he moves from the written Torah's prophetic record to the oral Torah's rabbinic record in the Babylonian Talmud *(Bavli),* the appeal to the "fully formed personality" of God with corporeal traits, attitudes, emotions, and actions is fundamentally the same: "God is Israel's counterpart" while remaining ineffable.[15] Likewise, when he proposes "a Christian telling of the Judaic tale," he attempts to explain to Christians "in Judaic terms" what "Israel" stands for, with its fusion of "the ethnic, the religious, the cultural, and the political." While he does draw parallels to Christian usage of Adam and the Suffering Servant, the basic appeal is an ethical one: Israel as the Suffering Servant in the Holocaust who maintains as intrinsic to her identity the possession of the land of Israel.[16] The ethical issue here is a matter of biblical justice, something that Christians can enter into with sympathy and imagination.

The second comment is to ask whether sympathy in the form of analogical imagination, while necessary and indispensable, is enough. Can we move from sympathy to empathy in the sense of truly entering into the experience of the other? John Dunne has remarked:

> The holy man of our time, it seems, is not a figure like Gotama or Jesus or Mohammed, a man who could found a world religion, but a figure like Gandhi, a man who passes over by sympathetic understanding from his own religion to other religions and comes back again with new insight to his own. Passing over and coming back, it seems, is the spiritual adventure of our time.[17]

This is surely the most difficult challenge in interreligious dialogue. It is hard enough to master one's own tradition in a significantly profound way. For Christians, as well as Jews, to come to some understanding of the tradition of rabbinic Judaism, one must grapple with the languages (ideally both biblical and rabbinic Hebrew and Aramaic), the intricacies of the texts (which demands the guidance of a rabbinic master), and the community of scholars/learners who argue about the texts. Nonetheless, true dialogue demands that we make the effort to participate in this postbiblical discourse.[18] This challenge carries another, even more urgent, namely that we cannot truly encounter each other as "other" until we recognize that "other" who, though silent to our deaf ears and invisible to our blind eyes, remains ineluctably present to our dialogue. As a matter of justice, we must "remember the poor" if our dialogue is to be authentic. The key is to be able to see the "real other" (the poor and oppressed on the underside of history) and to recognize that this "repressed other" is ourselves.[19]

The fourth and final condition Neusner mentions for the possibility of Jewish-Christian dialogue is that each shows the other respect, which in the tradition of the study of Torah (Talmud) means "a serious confrontation with the intellect and ideas of the other."[20] While this calls for a vigorous argument with the truth-claims of the other party, it also implies an openness to the truth of the other and a willingness to learn from the other. Cardinal Ratzinger affirms that, while there can be "no renunciation of truth," we still need to respect the beliefs of others and look for the truth in strange and unexpected places.

> Furthermore, I need to be willing to allow my narrow understanding of truth to be broken down. I shall learn my own truth better if I understand the other person and allow myself to be moved along the road to the God who is ever greater, certain that I never hold the whole truth about God in my own hands but am always a learner, on pilgrimage toward it, on a path that has no end.[21]

As a consequence, one must not only "look for what is positive in the other's beliefs," but also accept the justified criticism of the limitations of one's own religion. In a word, we need to learn from each other in a respectful and dialogic way.

To summarize, the conditions for the possibility of a true and authentic Jewish-Christian dialogue are: (1) a community of shared experience that neither invents nor dismisses the other party; (2) need for clarity about the issues that includes the kind of dialogue that is possible, the understanding of each other's terms, and conversation on the same issue; (3) recognition of difference that moves from the resources of one's own tradition through an act of analogical imagination to an understanding of what the other feels and affirms in the world of that other; (4) an attitude of respect that seriously engages the truth-claims of the other and is open to learn from them. Moving from the possibility to the actuality, is of course, no easy task. If it is both necessary and yet enormously difficult for a Christian to engage in an adequate way the classic texts of rabbinic Judaism, as indicated above, it is certainly difficult—though perhaps not equally so—for a Jew to engage the classic texts of orthodox Christianity. We turn now to the valiant attempt of Jacob Neusner to read the Gospel of Matthew with the avowed purpose "to foster religious dialogue among believers, Christian and Jewish alike." His goal is to make Christians better Christians and Jews better Jews by "establishing a discourse of autonomy for Judaism," i.e., by addressing the convictions of Christianity in Judaic terms.[22] One can only applaud the aim and intention of the author as it is necessary to read each other's texts for dialogue to happen, but there are difficulties along the way.

The Gospel of Matthew: An Example of the Necessity and Difficulty in Reading Each Other's Texts

In his talk with Jesus, Rabbi Neusner chooses the Gospel of Matthew, "Matthew's Jesus," in keeping with his understanding of the possibility of Jewish-Christian dialogue.

> Matthew's Jesus comes closest to an account of Jesus that a believing and practicing Jew can grasp in terms of Judaism. . . . An argument with Matthew's Jesus is plausible because there really is a shared Torah between us, so we can agree sufficiently on the main thing to disagree on other things.[23]

This is fair enough, though his dismissal of the historical Jesus as having no interest or relevance for believing Christians is misdirected, and his portrayal of John's Jesus as hating and loathing Jews is counterproductive. It is surprising, indeed ironic, that he does not see that John's Gospel is engaging in the same kind of argumentation that he is proposing, namely by starting from a shared agreement that "salvation is from the Jews" (John 4:22). But, these provisos aside, the main issue here is whether Rabbi Neusner is really talking with "Matthew's Jesus" and not with an invalid construct imposed on that Jesus by later history and subsequently proven to be unacceptable.

To put the matter simply, Neusner in sum buys into the individualizing and other-worldly spiritualizing view of Matthew's Jesus, which assuredly he could find in many Christian commentaries through the centuries. But, just as he feels that Matthew's Jesus ignores much that is in the Torah, so he ignores many texts in Matthew that would qualify and balance the above view, as a reading of Anthony Saldarini's study of Matthew's "Christian-Jewish community" attests. In fact, the contrast between the two interpretations could not be sharper. This is partly based in two different methods for assessing the situation at the time of Jesus. Neusner's criterion is the Torah of rabbinic Judaism.

> *My point is simple. By the truth of the Torah, much that Jesus said is wrong.* By the criterion of the Torah, Israel's religion in the time of Jesus was authentic and faithful, not requiring reform or renewal, demanding only faith and loyalty to God and the sanctification of life through carrying out God's will.[24]

Saldarini's approach takes a more critical, historical view of the first century that recognizes great diversity and overlap among several Judaisms and Christianities. Only later (fourth century and beyond) will they develop into the separate systems of Talmudic Judaism and orthodox Christianity. "The Jesus movement and rabbinic Judaism began as two Jewish reform programs. . . . At the level of lived religion, many Judaisms and Christianities found themselves in a variety of relationships, often much to the consternation of their more orthodox leaders."[25]

Neusner sees Jesus' teaching as running counter to who "we" are as the people Israel, a community of families. Jesus only speaks to the inner life of the individual, and the sense of community, family, home, the importance of the concretely lived experience of everyday life, is sadly omitted. Moreover, as Neusner sees it, Jesus instructs people to violate at least three of the ten commandments found in the following text: "You shall be holy, for I the LORD your God am holy. You shall each revere your mother and father, and you shall keep my sabbaths: I am the LORD your God" (Lev 19:2b-3). Neusner cites C. G. Montefiore: "Public justice is outside of his purview,"[26] in support of his view that Jesus has no interest in the social order. Needless to say, Saldarini's treatment counters all of these views. The titles of some of his chapters are indicative: "Matthew's People: Israel," "Matthew's Opponents: Israel's Leaders," "Matthew's Horizon: The Nations," "Matthew's Group of Jewish Believers-in-Jesus," "Matthew's Torah." By way of introduction to his chapter on Torah, he says: "Any attempt to portray Matthew as outside the Jewish discussion of how Jews ought to live ignores both Matthew's teaching of law and his presentation of Jesus."[27]

Neusner's choice of Matthew and his engagement of the text from a rabbinic viewpoint are much appreciated. Yet given his method of reading the text from later convictions, one might ask how he would perceive the later Christian interpretation of the text. Christians through the centuries have relied heavily on Matthew to affirm some of the very things Neusner finds lacking. As a matter of effective history, have Christians been completely wrong about understanding themselves as a people, a community, a family, who as such engage in public, not merely private, prayer and who strongly advocate observance of *all ten* commandments? Matthew's Gospel provides warrants for all of these understandings in subsequent Christian life. Yet there are tensions in Matthew that have left the Gospel open to diverse interpretations. While rejecting his individualizing and spiritualizing view, Neusner is certainly correct, and Saldarini agrees, that Matthew is a crucial text for Jewish-Christian dialogue. Saldarini puts it well:

> Matthew is at once the most Jewish of gospels in its traditions and interpretations and the most critical of gospels in its attacks on certain forms of Judaism. Matthew is an authentic witness both to the shared traditions that unite and to the deep hostilities that divide the Jewish and Christian communities. Most important, though, this gospel forces Christians to confront again and again their Jewish roots. . . . For Jews, the Gospel of Matthew understood positively testifies to the turbulent relations among various Jewish groups in the late first century and to the creative matrix that eventually produced rabbinic Judaism as the dominant tradition and way of living according to Torah.[28]

The Jewish roots of Christianity go back to Jesus himself in his historical life and mission. Matthew is one of the primary sources for knowledge about that Jesus. While it is true that Jesus' historical mission (as well as Matthew's view of it) had a focus that did not touch every issue that Rabbi Neusner raises in his talk with Jesus, it is not true either historically or in Matthew's narrative to characterize that mission as having no interest in the social order here and now. The lens of justice suggests quite otherwise. Saldarini, in the context of describing the social situation in Jesus' day, offers a clear and cogent summary of Jesus' historical mission that will be developed in Chapter 3.

> Jesus' central symbol of the kingdom of God gave the promise of a renewed covenantal relationship with God and a clearly articulated identity as God's people. It also promoted just social, political, and economic relationships within Israel and thus was an implied critique of the local elders and landowners, the Jerusalem leadership, and the Roman Empire.[29]

Given the difficulty yet necessity of reading each other's texts, it is important for the sake of clarity about the issues to probe more deeply into the different ways we can and do read/interpret the Hebrew Scriptures. To this we now turn.

Three Ways to Read/Interpret the Hebrew Scriptures

Perhaps the most important question that must be clearly stated in any Jewish-Christian dialogue is how one is reading and interpreting the sacred tradition, especially in this case the Hebrew Scriptures. Jews like Rabbi Neusner read "Torah" through rabbinic eyes. Christians like Cardinal Ratzinger read the "Old Testament" through New Testament (and subsequent patristic and conciliar) eyes. And scholars like Professor Saldarini read the "text" through hermeneutical, especially historical-critical, eyes. Such hermeneutic can include a more academic kind of consciousness and a more social and liberative kind of consciousness. What follows is a brief characterization of each optic.

Rabbinic Judaism only gradually emerged from the various movements present in the first century both before and after the destruction of Jerusalem and the Temple. The apparent demise of cult and priestly caste led rabbinic Judaism to seek to maintain levitical religion in another form. "In contrast to their patristic counterparts [who rejected routine levitical rituals], the post-70 C.E. founders of rabbinism aimed to perpetuate a levitical system."[30] The purpose is perhaps best seen in the divine command: "You therefore shall be holy, for I the LORD your God am holy" (Lev 19:2b). For Jacob Neusner, who frequently cites this text from Leviticus, the Mishnah (organized under Rabbi Judah the Prince ca. 200 C.E.) conveys "a single message. It is a message of a Judaism that answered a single encompassing question concerning the enduring sanctification of Israel, the people, the land, the way of life."[31] While the enduring sanctification of Israel was a major concern, it should also be recognized that the Mishnah and its successors are primarily collections of legal opinions *(halakhah)* that range over a wide variety of concerns in Jewish daily life. In any event, key to the eventual and continuing success of rabbinic Judaism is the doctrine of the oral as well as the written Torah, although the written Torah has precedence over the oral as the stable center of rabbinic Judaism.[32] This doctrine is based in the fact that there has never again arisen in Israel a prophet like Moses (Deut 34:10). This text in Deuteronomy, based on the affirmation that God knew Moses face to face, serves to demarcate the Pentateuch as the "Torah of Moses" from Joshua which begins the Prophets, "a later and inferior corpus of revelation."[33] Thus, priority is given to the five books of Moses in the Tanakh. In addition, according to the eighth principle of Maimonides (1135–1204), not only was the written Torah given to Moses on Sinai but also the entire Torah, i.e., the oral Torah of the rabbinic sages (principally Mishnah and Talmud). The important and central point is not so much the authorship of Moses as the unity and divinity of Torah.

Obviously, as Jon Levenson points out, this can create a certain tension or unresolved conflict with both traditional Christian exegesis and with contemporary biblical criticism. But it is important at the same time to recognize the uniqueness and validity of rabbinic Judaism as a way of reading the Hebrew Scriptures within its own structure and system.[34] It is also important to recognize other developments in the Jewish hermeneutical tradition such as Midrash, the art and process of interpretation present from the beginning and redacted from ca. 400 to 1200

C.E., which includes both *halakhah* (the "doing" of Torah) and *aggadah* (the homiletic and narrative "discourse" of Torah); the move to the *peshat,* or "plain-sense," method using the tools of secular learning to explain the text within its historical, literary, and linguistic context that flourished especially in the Middle Ages; the development of Kabbalistic mysticism which found its most influential expression with the *Zohar* ("radiance") ca. 1280 and became very influential in Galilee in the sixteenth century; and finally the development of charismatic communities around the *ṣaddîq* ("just" or "righteous"), the Hasidic holy man.[35]

Through all of this development, the fundamental question is not theoretical but always practical.

> So now, O Israel, what does the LORD your God require of you? Only to fear the LORD your God, to walk in all his ways, to serve the LORD your God with all your heart and with all your soul, and to keep the commandments of the LORD your God and his decrees that I am commanding you today, for your own well-being (Deut 10:12-13; cp. Mic 6:8).

That "now" transcends temporal limitations. It appeals to the heart of each member of the family of Israel. Pervasive is the message "the merciful God wants the heart."[36] The message from the Mishnah through the Palestinian and Babylonian Talmud is subservience to God's will expressed in Torah and embodied in "our sages of blessed memory," above all in "our Rabbi Moses." As it says: "Moses received Torah at Sinai and handed it on to Joshua, Joshua to elders, and elders to prophets. And prophets handed it on to the men of the great assembly. They said three things: 'Be prudent in judgment. Raise up many disciples. Make a fence for the Torah'" (*Mishnah Abot* 1:1). Thus, the definitive and authoritative Talmud of Babylonia affirms, as Neusner concludes, that "we can in the Torah know God's thoughts in God's words."[37] The study of the Hebrew Scriptures (*talmud* means "study" in Hebrew) is at one and the same time an act of worship, a spiritual, moral, and intellectual undertaking, and a fulfillment of religious obligation. This applies to God as well as to the sage because God is bound by the same rules. "That is because God made them to begin with, and made humanity in conformity with them."[38] So even God in heaven studies Torah.

Christian exegesis, in a somewhat parallel fashion to the development of rabbinic Judaism up to the seventh and eighth centuries and beyond into the Middle Ages, reads the "Old Testament" in the light of the "New Testament" as it is interpreted above all in the patristic and conciliar period (second to eighth centuries). A crucial difference between the traditions is the organization of each canon culminating in the final verse. The Hebrew canon (Tanakh) concludes with the inspired words of King Cyrus of Persia:

> Thus says King Cyrus of Persia: The LORD, the God of heaven, has given me all the kingdoms of the earth, and he has charged me to build him a house at Jerusalem, which is in Judah. Whoever is among you of all his people, may the LORD his God be with him! Let him go up (2 Chr 36:23).

The Christian "Old Testament" (Septuagint) concludes with the inspired words of the prophet Malachi:

> Remember the teaching of my servant Moses, the statutes and ordinances that I commanded him at Horeb for all Israel. Lo, I will send you the prophet Elijah before the great and terrible day of the LORD comes. He will turn the hearts of parents to their children and the hearts of children to their parents, so that I will not come and strike the land with a curse (Mal 4:4-6 LXX).[39]

Thus the Hebrew canon looks to the building of the Temple in Jerusalem, the possession of the land promised to eternal Israel as found in the Torah. The Christian canon, as interpreted in the New Testament, looks to John the Baptist as Elijah (Matt 11:7-15 par.; Luke 1:17) and to Jesus as bringing the teaching of Moses on Mount Sinai (Deut 5:1-3) and the prophecy of Elijah on the same mountain (1 Kgs 19:1-8) to fulfillment on the mountain of transfiguration (Matt 17:1-8 par.). In other words, the "end" of the Old Testament is a prophetic word that prepares for and finds its fulfillment in Christ as found in the New Testament. Although it would be anachronistic to ascribe to the authors of what we now call the "New Testament" such a canonical distinction, it is true that each author in distinctive ways did mine the only scripture they knew, the Hebrew Scriptures—usually in the form of the Greek translation known as the Septuagint—to support the view that in Jesus Israel's hopes have been fulfilled. Matthew is a classic example of this with his frequent citation of fulfillment texts.

Yet, as Saldarini notes, Matthew's way of following Jesus as a Jew loyal to the Law eventually lost out, beginning already in the second century. Indeed, it is not until Justin Martyr who died in Rome ca. 165 that the claim is explicitly made that Christians are "the true Israelite offspring *[genos]*."[40] But, prior to that, early-second-century authors in addition to Justin, for example Ignatius of Antioch, Barnabas, and 5 Ezra (chs. 1–2 of 2 Esdras added by an unknown Christian editor in the early- to mid-second century), were clearly claiming the Old Testament as a Christian book because for them Christianity had displaced Judaism. The situation was complex as various forms of *Jewish* Christianity existed well into the fourth and fifth centuries, but the view that eventually prevailed was that of these early-second-century authors.

The viewpoint is perhaps best illustrated by Christian claims to the Septuagint: "Despite its Jewish origin, what we today call the 'Septuagint,' at least as regards its designation, transmission, and use is first of all a *Christian* collection of writings."[41] In the view of Justin and others like him, the entire Bible consisted of "prophetic writings" foretelling Christ and his Church, in contrast to Judaism that considered Torah to be the determinative center and the prophets to be its interpreters.[42]

Justin's "dialogue," which is really an apologetic for ensuring that "the translation of the Seventy" is a Christian writing, turns into hostile polemic when he accuses his Jewish dialogue partners of both falsifying and misunderstanding these "prophetic writings." No wonder the rabbinic tradition stayed primarily with the Hebrew written text and the unassailable and unfalsifiable oral Torah given to Moses. In any event, the net result was that the Septuagint eventually came to be considered a Christian writing which only Christians could interpret correctly. Cardinal Ratzinger's claim that "if the Old Testament does not speak of Christ, it is not a Bible for Christians" resonates profoundly with Justin and subsequent orthodox writers. While this is a way to read the Old Testament that has a long history and is valid within the limits of its own perspective, one must still ask in the present climate of interreligious dialogue whether it is the only way to read the Old Testament. If a Christian can read the Old Testament and find there the God of Abraham, Isaac, and Jacob, the one God in whom Jews, Christians, and Muslims believe, the God of Israel whom Jesus prayed to as Abba, Father, is this not a Bible for Christians?

Modern hermeneutics, as the term implies, is a relatively recent phenomenon of interpretation beginning around the time of the "Enlightenment" (ca. eighteenth century) and continuing through the modern period into the contemporary "post-modern" scene. The catalyst for this move was the emancipation of reason from all forms of dogmatism, and it has had serious consequences for the way we read the Scriptures today. In its beginnings it tended to emphasize the diachronic, or historical-critical, over the synchronic, or canonical text taken as a literary whole.[43] It also tended to either bracket or denigrate faith commitments in favor of "scientific" knowledge that can be attained by human reason alone. In his fine book on the relationship between the traditional mode of biblical study (both Rabbinic and Christian) and the historical-critical method, Jon Levenson calls for a different approach: "The dignity both of traditional interpretation and of modern criticism depends on a careful separation of the two and a reengagement on new terms."[44] He is certainly correct that we need to understand and value each in relation to the other and that we should move beyond ignoring, disvaluing, or replacing the one with the other. On the one side, for genuine and profound dialogue to take place between Jews and Christians we cannot bracket our religious commitments and seek some kind of neutral common ground.[45] This is the strength in the positions of both Neusner and Ratzinger. On the other side, unlike them, Levenson sees a vital and necessary importance to be given to historical-critical methods within such a dialogue, not as a "trivializing antiquarianism" but as a "hermeneutic of retrieval" that includes reference to a "larger structure of meaning."[46]

The question of history and its relation to faith commitments can be viewed from two distinct but related perspectives. The one, symbolized by the Kantian approach to the Enlightenment, puts greater stress on the academic or theoretical resolution of the issue and relies more on seeking truth through explanatory methods. The other, symbolized by the Marxist approach to the Enlightenment, puts greater stress on the liberative or practical resolution of the issue and relies more on seeking truth through conscientization and social transformation.[47] Both address a crisis of meaning. The first as more theoretical seeks to find a rational solution to the problem, which here is the relation of history to faith. The second as more practical seeks to transform the conditions that create the concretely experienced realities of evil, especially of human suffering and oppression, which here means to create a new understanding of the faith through the eyes of the underside of history, as Gustavo Gutiérrez has so eloquently put it. Both perspectives make legitimate claims in the human quest for meaning and truth. Since the present work appeals to the historical Jesus as integral to the understanding of Christian faith, it is necessary to offer a fuller consideration of each in turn, first the "theoretical" and then the "practical."

Speaking in terms of a Christian understanding of covenantal relationship, our primary relationship to Jesus (or to the God revealed in Jesus: 2 Cor 5:16-21) is one of faith. Faith, even in the human sense, is an act of self-transcendence, of entrusting oneself to another, of taking a risk that goes beyond proof or evidence in a strictly scientific sense. Such an act is obviously based on the experience of the other person in the course of the lived experience of a relationship. Such an act is not unreasonable or even "blind," but as an act of self-transcendence it is a risk. It does entail the very real possibility that one could be mistaken or deceived, as only the continuing history of the relationship can reveal, but without the capacity and the willingness to transcend oneself and to entrust oneself to another person human life in its fullness cannot be lived. Human faith is analogous to religious faith as the latter affirms the priority of the divine initiative in the relationship. Nonetheless, even God takes a risk in calling us to faith since, as the histories of both Judaism and Christianity show, we can fail to remain faithful in the relationship. Religious faith also puts stress on the fact that the relationship is not only interpersonal ("I-Thou") but communal in nature and so includes the traditions and interpretations of the particular community to which one belongs. As such it is a complex reality. I describe *Christian* faith as "a graced but free human acceptance of God's self-communication in Christ as mediated by the Christian community."[48] We live within a tradition and, as Levenson affirms, must value the integrity of our own tradition as a totality. What then, within that faith tradition, is the function of historical knowledge as that knowledge is understood by contemporary historians?[49] It is my view that history functions in a subordinate but indispensable way in relation to our commitments in faith.

It is *subordinate* because the primary relationship is one of faith. Faith makes affirmations, for example about the character and activity of God, that simply transcend the limitations of scientific historical knowledge. To say that God raised Jesus from the dead is to make a statement that historical methods can neither affirm nor deny. A historian, by reason of the method employed and so staying within the limiting parameters of human experience as circumscribed by birth and death, can affirm that shortly after the death of Jesus certain of his disciples proclaimed that God raised him from the dead, which proclamation gave birth to the Christian Church that has had a continuing effect upon the course of human history. But a historian as such can neither verify nor falsify the claim itself. Whether God raised Jesus from the dead lies in the sphere of faith, which, in this view, is not reducible to the claims of science and/or history. Only if one held on a philosophical, not historical, basis that the only way one knows anything is through empirical, scientific knowledge would one be able to equate the two. But the view proposed here holds that faith is a kind of knowledge that is distinctive and unique and not reducible, except by analogy, to other kinds of knowledge.

Nonetheless, for Christian faith at least, historical knowledge is *indispensable* to faith. Here I would part company with anyone who would consider the historical Jesus to be unimportant, trivial, or superseded. Christian faith is deeply rooted in human history and human experience. We believe in one whose human life was *real,* and that includes all the ambiguities, trials, temptations that every human person is heir to by virtue of being born into this spatio-temporal world. If we had no knowledge of this Jesus, our faith would lose its rootedness in the personal history of Jesus and, as Ernst Kaesemann noted in his justly famous lecture of 1953 that inaugurated the so-called "new quest," we would be in danger of committing ourselves to "a mythological Lord."[50] Admittedly, our knowledge of the historical Jesus is limited and the methods are at times difficult to adjudicate, but on the theoretical level (Chapter 3 will develop what might be said in more specific terms) there are at least three values to be affirmed for such knowledge.

First, on a popular level, such knowledge has a direct and powerful appeal to the faithful whose faith urges them to know Jesus in humanly accessible ways, which is to say that Jesus is not just God who appears in human form but is truly and really a human being who, like us in all things (Heb 4:15), has personally experienced in solidarity with us our human joys and sorrows. Second, on a canonical level, such knowledge concretizes our faith-image of Jesus. Indeed, what would our image of Jesus be like if we had only the letters of Paul and not the four Gospels? And third, on a critical level, such knowledge exercises a negative control over false or inappropriate images of Jesus. Although the tendency is an ever-present danger in historical reconstruction, ideally historical knowledge can prevent us from creating Jesus in our image. It allows Jesus to be Jesus, to stand over against us and to challenge our presuppositions and our prejudices, such as anti-Judaism as a religious prejudice and anti-Semitism as a racial prejudice. To those who would claim Jesus, whether for a "right-wing" ideology that seeks to justify the status quo of systemic oppression or for a "left-wing" ideology that seeks to justify violent revolution, the best and indeed only answer is an appeal to what we know of Jesus historically. Such knowledge does not exhaust all we can say of Jesus in faith, but it does serve to control excesses and misdirections and to allow Jesus in his own historical uniqueness as a first-century Jew to stand as challenge and call.

This "theoretical" resolution of the issue moves us, then, immediately into the "practical" issue, i.e., the use of history in the various forms of liberation theology. Jon Levenson offers a rather trenchant critique of the liberationist use, or better co-optation, of the Exodus experience in ways that are anachronistic, ideological, and untrue to the Scriptures themselves. "The passionate demand for justice does indeed resound throughout the Hebrew Bible, but the identification of justice with equality is essentially a modern phenomenon and, in the hands of many modern exegetes, an impetus for gross anachronism."[51] He rightly distinguishes between a use of the Bible as "projection" that rewrites history according to one's own agenda and as "appropriation" that sees in the past analogies to one's present experience and concerns. To repeat, the proper use of historical criticism should function to control any attempt to re-create past figures in our own image or past events according to our own agenda. Levenson's view of the Exodus experience is insightful and will be discussed in Chapter 2, but for now the positive value of the liberationist lens in reading the Scriptures, both Jewish and Christian, needs consideration.

The fundamental question is, whose voice is being heard? Do Jews and Christians, in their traditional rabbinic and orthodox readings of Scripture, hear the voice of those on the underside of history, the oppressed, the marginalized, the despised? The voice of the economically poor? The voice of those excluded because of their race? The voice of women who have had the power of naming their own experience stolen from them? The voice, especially, of poor women of color who suffer the threefold oppression of class, sex, and race?[52] And finally, for the purpose of this work, the voice of the Jewish Jesus who walked in solidarity with his people and especially with those who were excluded and pushed to the margins? There are two inseparable dimensions to this question. The first is to allow and enable the poor and oppressed to find their own voice, to tell their own stories, to claim their own experience as authentic and valid. The second is to recognize and acknowledge that these same poor and oppressed are part of ourselves, frequently repressed, but present nonetheless even in their silence. So we must let the poor and oppressed speak for themselves and in ourselves.

The theological project of Gustavo Gutiérrez has been to recognize the poor as the "privileged bearers of the gospel" and so to enable them to become "the active, historical subjects of a new understanding of faith and theology."[53] It is the people at the base, the exploited, the despised, the marginated who must find their own voice. Theologians, pastoral agents, and others can assist and enable by their solidarity in the struggle, but finally they must give way to the voice of the people themselves. This involves a long process of maturation that best takes place in the context of popular ecclesial communities *(comunidades eclesiales de base),* which provide the two inseparable factors necessary for liberation: indigenization and conscientization, the people's recognition of themselves in their own history and experience, combined with the critical and imaginative appropriation of that memory in concrete and specific communal and political commitments that seek to transform the social reality. They do this primarily by telling their stories, retrieving the past in order to open up the possibility of an authentic future. As the poor and oppressed find their own voices and speak for themselves, they can no longer be patronized or romanticized. Their stories are real stories about real people with actual names and faces. It is the specificity and particularity of their experience in the stories they tell that can no longer be ignored or repressed. It is an "irruption of the poor in history," according to Gutiérrez.

This process of telling the stories within a communal context is common to all movements for liberation, but especially so in the women's movements that struggle to claim their own experience in the face of male domination. Given the androcentric and patriarchal character of both Judaism and Christianity, it is a matter of simple justice that women's voices be heard. Justice, as will be seen in Jesus' own historical mission, demands an open and faithful inclusivity. Judith Plaskow, discussing what it means to be fully and completely Jewish, puts it this way: "Only when those who have had the power of naming stolen from us find our voices and begin to speak will Judaism become a religion that includes all Jews—will it truly be a Judaism of women and men." And later: "Only a Jewish community that permits and desires its members to be present in their particularity and totality can know in its fullness the relationship to God that it claims as its center."[54] The tools for this "transformation of Judaism" within a communal context are historiography, midrash, and liturgy. History is essential because the present grows out of the past, but history must be approached with suspicion as well as remembrance in order to liberate the biblical text from its own participation in oppression.[55] The right to tell one's story in a communal setting is the most crucial tool in this process of liberation. If Jews rightly object to being dispossessed of their own story, Jewish feminists object to the silencing or ignoring of women's history, which they see as essential to the whole story. Midrash has been the classic means to tell the story. "The open-ended process of writing midrash—simultaneously serious and playful, imaginative, metaphoric—has easily lent itself to feminist use."[56] Reading and writing in the margins, in "the white spaces between the letters in the Torah," they tell the stories of Miriam, of Eve and Lilith, of Sarah, of Dina and the Canaanite woman (Gen 34:1). "The discovery of women in our history can feed the impulse to create midrash; midrash can seize on history and make it religiously meaningful. Remembering and inventing together help recover the hidden half of Torah, reshaping Jewish memory to let women speak."[57] The celebration in liturgy and ritual of women's experience as integral to the life of the whole community is the third tool of true liberation and transformation, for it is here in symbolic, bodily form that the central experiences and values are expressed and communicated.

If, then, we can allow the poor and oppressed to speak for themselves and to celebrate their own experience, we must equally and at a more profound level allow them to speak in ourselves. We must be willing to recognize and accept the poor and oppressed "other" as existing in ourselves, as part of who we are as a people on all levels of our human lives: religious, social, cultural, ethnic, political, economic. Joerg Rieger has made a strong case that this is the challenge to theology in the twenty-first century. He develops this within the framework of Christian theology and draws heavily on the works of Frederick Herzog as representative of the southern United States and of Gustavo Gutiérrez as representative of Latin America (Peru) in order to show

how his thesis works out in both the northern and southern hemispheres. But what he says is surely applicable to all forms of dialogue and especially to Jewish-Christian dialogue. Herzog puts the shift in perspective this way: "Liberation theology begins as the poor begin to listen to each other before God. Liberation theology continues as we listen to the poor before God."[58] If the marginalized "other," who have actual names and real stories, are not consciously present, can our dialogue be authentic? Both the traditional concern for "texts" and the modern concern for the "self" will undergo transformation through such an encounter. As always, the key is the interaction of authority and power. To be able to determine the identity and interests of another (authority) is to exercise a societal control that produces obedience (power). When the "other" is subdued and turned into an object to be manipulated, both authority and power are corrupted. Whether the focus is on the authority of the "text" or on the authority of the "self," the voice of the "other" on the underside of history is effectively shut out and repressed. To encounter that voice is to be concerned not only about the human "other" but more fundamentally about the divine "Other." The question both now and at the time of Jesus' proclamation of the reign of God is one of theo-praxis: What is God doing? It is a question of God's own authority and power.

In a discussion of "Jesus and Power," Herzog asks what difference it makes to Christian theology that Jesus was a Jew, that a Jewish understanding of his selfhood could be significant.

> Would it be possible for Jews and Christians to dialogue on Jesus as a Jew not yet caught up in Christian individualism? Would it perhaps be possible for Christians to see how he embodied the corporateness of Jewish selfhood in a new way so that the outcast and oppressed were also acknowledged as part of the self?[59]

He argues that Jesus was trying to reconstitute power, that to create a power balance within the corporate reality of Israel by the inclusion of the excluded affects not only the corporate consciousness of Israel's identity but also of human experience as such.

> It is their corruption of power that enables human beings to prey on each other. Underlying the power corruption is the exclusion of the other from one's selfhood. The Jesus event acknowledges the other as part of the self, especially the marginal other. The commandment to love the other as oneself is not an invitation to love an alien other, but finally to discover the other as co-constitutive of one's self. This awareness of one's identity in corporate selfhood emerges in the church in the wrestle with the Jesus event at the ground level of Christian origins in Judaism.[60]

This is not just a question of Jesus' praxis of identification with the oppressed but of Jesus' own identity as the "other." According to Rieger, Christian theologians today are "blind guides" to the extent that they ignore or repress that identity; in Gutiérrez's terms, of the God who became poor in Christ.

Terry Veling advocates the need for a "marginal hermeneutics," at least for small, intentional Christian communities. This coheres well with the experience of Jewish feminists like Judith Plaskow and with the proposal of Joerg Rieger. "Theology must transcend the typical blindness of the modern self and the ecclesial texts by reading between the lines and venturing into that which, from the perspective of selves and texts, exists only in repressed form."[61] Interestingly, Veling finds the hermeneutic for "living in the margins" in the Jewish interpretative tradition. Using the metaphor of the "book," he evokes the tension between trust and suspicion, between belonging in the pages of the book and non-belonging in the sense of not finding oneself in the pages of the book. "In other words, the book represents our radical belonging to tradition; absence and exile represent our alienation from the book, and the margins of the book represent where new interpretation and the writing of tradition occur."[62] Marginal writing, then, seeks to overcome the experience of exile by finding the open spaces in between the letters and in the margins where God continues to speak to those whom God has chosen, women and men, poor and rich, black and white. The Jews as the people of Israel have in ways inseparable from Christian identity been that "other" who have always made their presence felt.[63] Jacob-Israel has continued to wrestle with God and humans through the centuries. Christians wrestle with that same God, the divine "Other," who is the only absolute but who is inseparably connected to and involved with the human "other." They must do so if they would engage in authentic dialogue with their Jewish origins and with the unique people who continue to embody those origins.

Is There a Key Issue in the Jewish-Christian Dialogue?

Of the many issues that could emerge in a review of the massive amount of literature on Jewish-Christian dialogues, three will be considered briefly here: (1) a negative issue from the past: supersessionism; (2) a positive issue for the future: the classic criterion for the messianic age; and (3) a convergent issue that brings past and future together into new possibilities for the present: the biblical understanding of righteousness and justice as covenantal fidelity.

Mary Boys makes the strong case that the fundamental issue on all levels of Christian life—exegesis, theology, liturgy, catechetics—is supersessionism.

> Supersessionism, from the Latin, *supersedere* (to sit upon, to preside over), is the theological claim that Christians have replaced Jews as God's people because the Jews rejected Jesus. Three interrelated claims are inherent in supersessionism: (1) the New Testament fulfills the Old Testament; (2) the church replaces the Jews as God's people; and (3) Judaism is obsolete, its covenant abrogated.[64]

I call this a negative issue from the past not because it does not continue to be a widespread conviction among Christians, especially on a popular level, but because it should now be superseded. Nonetheless, such a claim must address two related questions. First, is anti-Judaism and/or anti-Semitism intrinsic to Christian self-identity; second, is some form of supersessionism intrinsic to monotheistic religions, as exemplified perhaps in the Hebrew Bible?

The terms "anti-Judaism" and "anti-Semitism," though in need of much nuance, provide a common and useful distinction. The latter could include other Semites such as Arabs, but as a negative and racist designation it was first used explicitly in reference to Jews in the nineteenth century. The first is a theological and apologetic term that in some form rejects the religious claims of one or other form of "Judaism" without necessarily rejecting the Jewish people as a racial or ethnic group. Anti-Judaism is, then, a term more appropriate for discussing the New Testament materials and the history that lies behind them. Yet it should not be forgotten that such anti-Judaism did provide warrants for anti-Semitism. George Smiga, in discussing Douglas Hare's threefold classification of anti-Judaism as respectively "prophetic," "Jewish-Christian," and "Gentilizing," makes the point that the term anti-Judaism as applied to the New Testament "implies a normative Judaism from which to deviate." So he retains the term "only for Hare's third category in which the Jewish people as a whole are seen to be rejected by God"; i.e., not in a racial but in a theological sense. For the first two categories, Smiga prefers the term "polemic," both "prophetic" and "subordinating." Also, the distinction between Jewish and Gentile needs more nuance as there were varying types of Jewish/Gentile Christianity during this period. Hence, with the focus on polemic, the following distinctions are employed by Smiga: (1) "prophetic polemic," an intra-communal criticism of certain abuses, e.g., of observance of Torah or of ritual practices in the Temple, without subverting the symbols themselves; (2) "subordinating polemic," a subtle distinction from the prophetic but one that moves in the direction of subordinating some symbols to a new value or redefining and/or re-symbolizing the very identity of Israel, e.g., Christ as embodying in a new way the values of Torah; (3) "abrogating anti-Judaism," the view that Israel has been rejected or that the "old" Israel has been eliminated and replaced by the "new" Israel. The advantage of such classification is that it recognizes much greater diversity, flexibility, and complexity in early Christian attitudes during the period of formative Judaism from intra-Jewish disputes to arguments over symbols to the abrogation of Judaism in a supersessionist sense. Thus we should not read back into this period our modern understandings of Judaism and Christianity as religions, and we should be open to the possibility that supersessionism is not intrinsic or necessary to Christian self-identity.[65]

As to whether supersessionism is inherent in monotheistic religions with their strong claims about the character of the deity, Jon Levenson affirms a biblical connection.

> Without such precedents as the partial dispossession of Ishmael by Isaac and of Esau by Jacob in the Hebrew Bible—the only Bible he knew—Paul and the Church's partial dispossession of the Jews could hardly have been conceived. Christian supersessionism is much indebted to the narrative dynamics of the Jewish foundational story and, ironically, cannot be grasped apart from the story it claims to supersede.[66]

As history shows, strong claims about one's possession of the truth lead to equally strong claims about one's superiority. Yet neither rabbinic Judaism, with its recognition that there are many ways to salvation, is inherently supersessionist nor orthodox Christianity, with its recognition that the Spirit of God works in mysterious and unknown ways in all people. Jewish-Christian dialogue cannot be fully effective, then, unless it includes dialogue with all the world religions, especially with Islam.[67] Only then can the tendency toward supersessionism be adequately recognized and repudiated.

The question of supersessionism inevitably raises the question of whether the messianic age has come. I call this a positive issue for the future because both Jews and Christians, though in differing ways, can agree that the full and public manifestation of the messianic age has not yet arrived. At the end of his exhaustive study on community in the Bible, Paul Hanson affirms as the biblical legacy that the classic criterion for the messianic age persisted into early Christianity and rabbinic Judaism: "God's reign would be inaugurated when God's sovereignty was acknowledged and God's will was obeyed by all."[68]

For Jews, as Jacob Neusner has shown, the triumph and challenge of Christianity stimulated the sages of the Palestinian and Babylonian Talmud to focus on the Messiah theme but within the context of the Mishnah. Put simply and in summary form, the answer to "who" is a son of David born when the Temple was destroyed and so the provider of a better fate, one who fully embodies the wisdom of the sages. The answer to "when" is "whenever you want" (*Y. Taanit* 1:1, cited by Neusner), which means that the answer to "how" is perfect fulfillment of God's will in Torah, Israel's power to reform itself through repentance and observance of sabbath. "God's will in heaven and the sage's words on earth—both constituted Torah."[69] Thus the Messiah, the savior of Israel, will be the humblest sage, the one who perfectly fulfills Torah. Pinchas Lapide appeals to eleven biblical prophecies that must be visibly and publicly manifest to say that the messianic age has arrived. "No Torah faithful Jew can believe in the beginning of the messianic age until the 11 prophecies mentioned above are visibly fulfilled on the public stage of world history."[70] The basic theme of these prophecies centers around the peace and harmony of all peoples and the whole of creation with the God of Israel in Jerusalem. In the well-known text of *B. Sanhedrin* 97b, this all depends on "repentance and good deeds," i.e., on perfect observance of Torah.

For Christians, as Ulrich Luz makes clear, there is a difference between the Jewish expectation of a theo-political Messiah and the Christian understanding, in the light of his death and resurrection, that *Jesus* is the Christ. Indeed, whatever diverse expectations and understandings of messianic hope may have existed in the time of Jesus, the attribution of the title "Christ" to him takes on an entirely different meaning in view of the cross. The great apologetic task of the early Christians, clearly exemplified in the Gospel of Mark, was not to claim that Jesus was the Messiah or even the Son of God—others had claimed as much—but to claim that *this crucified man* was Messiah and Son of God. The crucifixion of Jesus means that the messianic age has not yet arrived except by way of proleptic anticipation in the resurrection. All the New Testament authors, by their constant exhortations to follow in the way of Jesus, demonstrate the fact that the resurrection impels us forward to do the will of God in the hope and expectation that God's reign will be finally and fully realized (e.g., 1 Cor 15:20-28, which is the culmination of a long paraenetic section exhorting the Corinthians to live what they believe).

> Jews and Christians are called to preserve and demonstrate his messianic hope for all the world. In the words of Hans-Werner Bartsch: "The question concerning the right relationship between Jews and Christians is not whether Israel wishes to accept Christ as its Messiah, but rather the opposite, whether Christendom will acknowledge that it has been accepted by grace into the covenant between God and Israel. It is Christendom that should be asked by Israel whether it wishes to share in Israel's hope that God may in the end be everything to everyone (1 Cor 15:28). . . . As Christians we must allow ourselves to be missionized by Israel, so that we may recapture this hope and from it learn to understand our existence anew."[71]

That Christians have been accepted by grace into the covenant between God and Israel is the key issue around which this book centers and which, it is hoped, may signal a certain convergence of Jews and Christians that opens up new possibilities for the dialogue. The biblical understanding of righteousness and justice as covenantal fidelity is the subject of Chapter 2. On that basis, Chapter 3 asks whether Jesus' own proclamation of the power and authority of God's reign is primarily a matter of such justice. The focal and key issue is thus not Christology, whether Christians are right about Jesus, but theology, whether Jesus was right about God.[72]

Notes

[1] Mary C. Boys, *Has God Only One Blessing? Judaism as a Source of Christian Self-Understanding* (Mahwah, N.J.: Paulist Press, 2000) 6. The guiding image of the book is a "new posture" for Ecclesia and Synagoga as sculpted by Paula Mary Turnbull (photo on p. 246): "Christian iconography of the Middle Ages provides a vivid image of rivalry in the figures 'Synagoga' and 'Ecclesia.' . . . Typically, they portray Ecclesia as standing erect and triumphant, symbol of the church of the victorious Christ. Synagoga, in contrast, is a conquered figure, symbol of Judaism's defeat and obsolescence. God had only one blessing to give—and now Ecclesia, not Synagoga, received it" (5).

[2] Ibid., 8; emphasis in original.

[3] Ibid., 8–10. Boys offers a summary account of the history of Jewish-Christian relations on 39–74, a contrast in summary form of the conventional account of Christian origins on 76–9, and her alternate account on 82–5. For similar accounts of the history on the Jewish side see Jules Isaac, *The Teaching of Contempt: Christian Roots of Anti-Semitism,* trans. Helen Weaver and biographical intro. by Claire Huchet Bishop (New York: Holt, Rinehart and Winston, 1964). The appendix offers a summary list of propositions from his earlier and influential *Jésus et Israël* (Paris: 1948). Isaac had a profound influence on Pope John XXIII and thus on Vatican II's decree *Nostra Aetate.* On the Roman Catholic side see Edward H. Flannery, *The Anguish of the Jews: Twenty-Three Centuries of Antisemitism,* rev. and updated (Mahwah, N.J.: Paulist Press, 1985); Rosemary Radford Ruether, *Faith and Fratricide: The Theological Roots of Anti-Semitism* (New York: Seabury Press, 1974); John T. Pawlikowski, *What Are They Saying About Christian-Jewish Relations?* (New York: Paulist Press, 1980); and, recently, James Carroll, *Constantine's Sword: The Church and the Jews: A History* (Boston: Houghton Mifflin, 2001), which has stimulated a great deal of discussion on the issues.

[4] Flannery, *The Anguish of the Jews,* 1, 295. Pawlikowski, writing in 1979, is more optimistic. While at that time the Jewish-Christian dialogue seems to have slowed down, Pawlikowski contradicts any claim that it is dead and sees rather an opportunity to move beyond the initial euphoria to a discussion of the deeper

doctrinal and moral issues. "The dialogue will not reach maturity until Christians and Jews are able to candidly discuss their differences on all levels and genuinely profit from a grasp of the unique elements in each other's tradition" (*What Are They Saying?* ix). His book seeks to delineate some of the major issues: the charge of deicide and the New Testament as anti-Semitic; the theology of the covenant; Jewish views on Christianity; Jesus and the Pharisaic tradition; Judaism's historic claim to the land; the Nazi Holocaust. Of course, these are discussions among scholars and do not invalidate the view of Boys and Flannery on the lack of sensitivity to these issues on the part of Christians as a whole. Nonetheless, in the last twenty years (1980s to the present), there has been a veritable explosion of literature on Jewish-Christian relations as witnessed by one publisher among others, namely the Stimulus Books Series from Paulist Press.

[5] Boys, *Has God Only One Blessing?* 247–66.

[6] Jacob Neusner, *Telling Tales: Making Sense of Christian and Judaic Nonsense: The Urgency and Basis for Judeo-Christian Dialogue* (Louisville: Westminster/John Knox Press, 1993) 5; 6; 21–2, n. 2, which gives his reasons for excluding Islam, Germany, and the State of Israel at the present time.

[7] Ibid. 22, n. 2; 23.

[8] Joseph Cardinal Ratzinger, *Many Religions—One Covenant: Israel, the Church and the World,* trans. Graham Harrison (San Francisco: Ignatius Press, 1999) 19, 45–6.

[9] Ibid., 18. In an address to a Jewish-Christian meeting in Jerusalem in February 1994, he puts it this way: "The Catechism as a book of faith proceeds from the conviction that the Jesus of the Gospels is also the only true historical Jesus" (ibid., 29; his talk was based on the 1992 *Catechism of the Catholic Church*).

[10] Neusner, *Telling Tales,* 86–9. The reference is to Samuel Sandmel, *We Jews and Jesus* (New York: Oxford University Press, 1965). Neusner, in both *Telling Tales* and *A Rabbi Talks with Jesus* (Montreal/Ithaca, N.Y.: McGill-Queen's University Press, 2000), frequently refers to the question of the historical Jesus as "trivial," "beside the point," "without foundation," etc.

[11] Cited from *Mishnah Abot* 5:26 in Barry W. Holtz, ed., *Back to the Sources: Reading the Classic Jewish Texts* (New York: Simon & Schuster, 1984) 185. The citation is in the article by Holtz entitled "Midrash." He comments: "All the rabbis would subscribe to a doctrine of the eternal interpretability of Torah and we might say that if there is any one dogma of rabbinic Judaism it is that *everything is contained therein*" (emphasis in original).

[12] Neusner, *Telling Tales,* 104.

[13] Ibid., 106. He emphasizes the role of stories: "What moves me, as distinct from what persuades me, is the story the other person tells" (106–7). He offers as an example Mary's unique relationship to God (which is certainly not the center of Christian faith, though important), to which he finds an analogy in the story of Rachel in *Lamentations Rabbah.* "What I find striking in this story is how very much Rachel is like Mary (or Mary like Rachel): that is, the one who succeeds when all other intervention fails" (115). Would not this appeal to analogies in the stories we tell work for the historical Jesus as well; e.g., the binding of Isaac (the *aqedah*) on a mountain called Moriah (Gen 22:2) and the crucifixion of Jesus at a place called Golgotha (Mark 15:22)?

[14] William James, *The Varieties of Religious Experience* (New York: Collier, 1961) 390–1: "When we survey the whole field of religion, we find a great variety in the thoughts that have prevailed there; but the feelings on the one hand and the conduct on the other are almost always the same, for Stoic, Christian, and Buddhist saints are practically indistinguishable in their lives. The theories which Religion generates, being thus variable, are secondary; and if you wish to grasp her essence, you must look to the feelings and the conduct as being the more constant elements."

[15] Neusner, *Telling Tales,* 124, 126–8, 130–8.

[16] Ibid., 145, 140, 157–8. Similarly, Edward Flannery in addressing anti-Zionism as "the third wave of antisemitism in this century" finds at its core a fallacy and a refusal. "The fallacy consists in defining Jewishness as *only* a religion, not a peoplehood or a nation, whereas it is essentially all of these; the refusal, in not allowing Jews to define themselves. . . . For the committed Jew, an attack on Zionism, on Israel, is an attack on his Jewishness and his Judaism" (*The Anguish of the Jews,* 267, 268; emphasis in original).

[17] John S. Dunne, *The Way of All the Earth* (New York: Macmillan, 1972) ix.

[18] This reflection came from reading the very accessible collection of essays edited by Barry W. Holtz, *Back to the Sources*. The whole book is designed to encourage the reader to plunge into the classic Jewish texts. See, for example, Robert Goldenberg, "Talmud," who at the end offers suggestions on why and how to study Talmud (163–75). Jon Levenson puts it strongly: "The disastrous effects on both Wellhausen and Eichrodt of ignorance of literature in postbiblical Hebrew underscore a truism that much of the scholarly world still evades: one cannot be a competent scholar of the Christian Bible without a solid command of rabbinic literature and rabbinic Hebrew (and Aramaic). Hebrew did not die on the cross." Jon D. Levenson, *The Hebrew Bible, the Old Testament, and Historical Criticism* (Louisville: Westminster/John Knox Press, 1993) 21.

[19] Joerg Rieger, *Remember the Poor: The Challenge to Theology in the Twenty-First Century* (Harrisburg, Pa.: Trinity Press International, 1998). See my review in *Theological Studies* 60 (September 1999) 566–7. Interestingly, Rabbi David Hartman remarks with regard to the State of Israel: "We have come home, yet to a home which does not offer us security and serenity, but forces us to meet the other." Rabbi David Hartman, "Judaism Encounters Christianity Anew," *Visions of the Other: Jewish and Christian Theologians Assess the Dialogue,* ed. Eugene J. Fisher (Mahwah, N.J.: Paulist Press, 1994) 74.

[20] Neusner, *A Rabbi Talks with Jesus,* 29. On pp. 27–30 he offers "rules for a shared and fair debate" invoking the very Jewish tradition of arguing with God (Abraham, Moses, Jeremiah, Job): "In my religion, argument forms a mode of divine service, as much as prayer" (24).

[21] Ratzinger, *Many Religions,* 109–10. Ratzinger distinguishes mystical types of religion from theistic types and also a pragmatic model of religion (orthopraxis) from a theistic model. He feels only the latter is appropriate for Jewish-Christian dialogue. In the course of his discussion of Judaism and Christianity, he remarks: "Israel may find it impossible to see Jesus as the Son of God as Christians do; but it is not impossible for them to see him as the Servant of God

who carries the light of his God to the nations" (104). Rabbi Neusner would say that Israel herself fulfills that role.

[22] Neusner, *A Rabbi Talks with Jesus*, 4–5, 12, 15–16.

[23] Ibid., 8.

[24] Ibid., 5.

[25] Anthony J. Saldarini, *Matthew's Christian-Jewish Community* (Chicago: University of Chicago Press, 1994) 25. At the end of the book he comments: "The historical facts of the overlapping of Christianity and Judaism, extending into the fourth and even seventh century in the East, undercut the recent theological thesis of Jacob Neusner that the essential core of Christianity and of (formative, rabbinic) Judaism were present and effective in the first century" (297, n. 9). He refers to Jacob Neusner, *Jews and Christians: The Myth of a Common Tradition* (London: SCM Press, 1991) ch. 2.

[26] Neusner, *A Rabbi Talks with Jesus*, 44, citing C. G. Montefiore, *The Synoptic Gospels* (New York: Ktav Publishing House, 1968; original 1927) 71. Neusner concludes that this is why he would not have followed Jesus. "'Public justice is outside of his purview'—and so too is that entirety of eternal Israel in which I have my being" (52).

[27] Saldarini, *Matthew's Christian-Jewish Community*, 124. In his conclusions, he comments: "This study concludes that the Gospel of Matthew addresses a deviant group within the Jewish community in greater Syria, a reformist Jewish sect seeking influence and power (relatively unsuccessfully) within the Jewish community as a whole" (198).

[28] Ibid., 205.

[29] Ibid., 39.

[30] William Scott Green, "The Hebrew Scriptures in Rabbinic Judaism," *Rabbinic Judaism: Structure and System*, Jacob Neusner (Minneapolis: Fortress Press, 1995) 33.

[31] Neusner, *Rabbinic Judaism*, 226.

[32] "Torah" has many meanings: the *sefer* Torah or sacred scroll of the Pentateuch in Hebrew consonants as the place of God's Presence; the written Torah of Moses (the five books of the Pentateuch); the entire Hebrew canon or Tanakh (Law, Prophets, and Writings); the oral Torah given to Moses as well on Sinai and found in the entire rabbinic tradition from Mishnah to its fulfillment in the Babylonian Talmud *(Bavli);* and so "the generative symbol, the total, exhaustive expression of the system as a whole," i.e., "a distinctive and well-defined worldview and way of life." Torah is what one does and ultimately leads to salvation. Ibid., 45–6. Green, "The Hebrew Scriptures," 37, describes the scroll's sanctity as a new sacred center: "As an artifact, the Torah scroll, with its holy and allegedly unchanged and changeless writing, formed the requisite stable center for rabbinism's system of piety. In the absence of the Temple and its Holy of Holies, the scroll and its writing became for ancient rabbis primary repositories and conveyers of social legitimacy, cultural authenticity, and religious meaning."

[33] The text draws on some of the comments of Levenson, "The Eighth Principle of Judaism and the Literary Simultaneity of Scripture," *The Hebrew Bible*, 62–5, 74, 76–9.

[34] Neusner, *Rabbinic Judaism,* vii–ix, summarizes the book. "We deal, of course, with only one Judaism, delineated by its authoritative writings ('canon'), defined by its generative myth and symbol ('dual Torah,' 'the Torah'), formulated by its holy men ('our sages of blessed memory'), addressed to its version of 'Israel' ('children of Abraham and Sarah,' sole heir and continuator of the Israel of whom Scripture speaks). Other, competing Judaic religious systems took shape both before, at the same time as, and after the formation of the one that is under study in this book. Each defined its Israel, dictated its ethics, and formulated its ethos. But none endured in Israel, the people, through all future time into our own day as did Rabbinic Judaism" (viii).

[35] In the book edited by Barry W. Holtz, *Back to the Sources,* the various authors give a clear and readable account of these developments. For a parallel history of Christianity and rabbinic Judaism that could give more attention to the interaction of the two religions over the centuries, see Hershel Shanks, ed., *Christianity and Rabbinic Judaism: A Parallel History of Their Origins and Early Development* (Washington, D.C.: Biblical Archaeology Society, 1992).

[36] Neusner, *Rabbinic Judaism,* 131. This is a theme that courses through the entire book.

[37] Ibid., 205. Neusner's translation of *Mishnah Abot* 1:1-9 is on pp. 51–2, from which the cited verse is taken.

[38] Ibid., 200. Neusner cites the Babylonian Talmud *Baba Mesia* 86A and concludes: "The critical point in this story comes at three places. First, God and the sages in heaven study the Torah in the same way the Torah is studied on earth. Second, God is bound by the same rules of rationality that prevail down here. Third, the sage on earth studies the way God does in heaven, and God calls up to heaven sages whose exceptional acuity and perspicacity are required on the occasion" (201).

[39] Nahum M. Sarna, "The Authority and Interpretation of Scripture in Jewish Tradition," *Understanding Scripture: Explorations of Jewish and Christian Traditions of Interpretation,* ed. Clemens Thoma and Michael Wyschogrod (Mahwah, N.J.: Paulist Press, 1987) 11–12, calls attention to this difference of the canons in his discussion of "inner biblical exegesis."

[40] Saldarini, *Matthew's Christian-Jewish Community,* 226, n. 3, citing Justin Martyr, *Dialogue with Trypho* 123, 135. See the whole discussion of "Matthew within First-Century Judaism" (11–26), especially his treatment of Jewish-Christian relationships (18–20) and later of "Israel" (28).

[41] Martin Hengel, "The Septuagint as a Collection of Writings Claimed by Christians: Justin and the Church Fathers before Origen," *Jews and Christians,* ed. Dunn, 39 (emphasis in original).

[42] Ibid., 43 (cf. n. 20). Hengel's article (39–83) is a brilliant review of this period in early Church history.

[43] In *Christology as Narrative Quest* (Collegeville: The Liturgical Press, 1997), I advocate the primacy of narrative, the text in its literary character as story, over historical, philosophical, or experiential affirmations, which I see as integral and necessary but subordinate to the story as the primary mode of God's self-communication, i.e., revelation.

[44] Levenson, *The Hebrew Bible,* xiv–xv.

[45] Ibid., 84, where he states in advance his conclusion to chapter 4 on Jews and Christians in biblical studies: "to the extent that Jews and Christians bracket their religious commitments in the pursuit of biblical studies, they meet not as Jews and Christians, but as something else, something not available in the days of Nachmanides and Pablo Christiani." The latter reference is to "the Great Disputation between Rabbi Moses ben Nachman (Nachmanides) and the convert Pablo Christiani in Barcelona in 1263" (82).

[46] Ibid., 99. He concludes: "Historical criticism has indeed brought about a new situation in biblical studies. The principal novelty lies in the recovery of the Hebrew Bible as opposed to the Tanakh and the Old Testament affirmed by rabbinic Judaism and Christianity, respectively. Jews and Christians can, in fact, meet as equals in the study of this new/old book, but only because the Hebrew Bible is largely foreign to both traditions and precedes them. . . . But unless historical criticism can learn to interact with other senses of scripture—senses peculiar to the individual traditions and not shared between them—it will either fade or prove to be not a meeting ground of Jews and Christians, but the burial ground of Judaism and Christianity, as each tradition vanishes into the past in which neither had as yet emerged" (105).

[47] I have treated the issue of the relationship between the Jesus of history and the Christ of faith at greater length elsewhere. See Michael L. Cook, *The Historical Jesus* (Chicago: Thomas More Press, 1986) 65–106. Also, Michael L. Cook, *The Jesus of Faith* (Mahwah, N.J.: Paulist Press, 1981) 1–34. For an interesting recent discussion of differing approaches in biblical interpretation by two Lutherans, one a Church historian and the other a biblical scholar, see Terence E. Fretheim and Karlfried Froehlich, *The Bible as Word of God in a Post-Modern Age* (Minneapolis: Fortress Press, 1998) and my review in *Theological Studies* 60 (1999) 575–6. The difference revolves around the weight one gives to the authority of the Bible vis-à-vis contemporary insights and concern. Froehlich in his response to Fretheim observes: "Apologetic zeal gives in too quickly to the instincts of contemporary mentalities without allowing room for their critique by the biblical witness" (131).

[48] See my article, "Faith," *The HarperCollins Encyclopedia of Catholicism,* ed. Richard P. McBrien (New York: Harper San Francisco, 1995) 510–5.

[49] Van A. Harvey, *The Historian and the Believer: A Confrontation Between the Modern Historian's Principles of Judgment and the Christian's Will-to-Believe* (Toronto: Macmillan, 1966; reissued by Philadelphia: Westminster Press, 1984) still remains one of the best analyses of what historians actually "do" when they do history, especially with regard to the "texture" or quality of assent that recognizes the limitations of the methods employed and so will not seek to elicit a "heavier" kind of assent than the evidence can bear.

[50] Ernst Kaesemann, "The Problem of the Historical Jesus," *Essays on New Testament Themes* (London: SCM Press, 1964) 1–46.

[51] Levenson, *The Hebrew Bible,* 133. Toward the end of his chapter "Exodus and Liberation," he comments on this "liberationist supersessionism" in even stronger terms: "In dispossessing the Jews of what they consider their own story, in denying the natural familial character of early Israel altogether *even in the Hebrew Bible itself,* this type of liberationism, whether intentionally or not,

taps into wells of Christian Jew-hatred that are as deep as they are ancient" (157–8, emphasis in original).

[52] I develop this more fully in a chapter on the "Mexican American Experience" in *Christology as Narrative Quest,* 176–211. A basic theme is that no one of us is free until poor women of color are free, for they embody really and symbolically the threefold oppression of class, sex, and race that imprisons all of us within the social and political reality of oppression.

[53] Gutiérrez's view is analyzed in Michael L. Cook, "Jesus from the Other Side of History: Christology in Latin America," *Theological Studies* 44 (June 1983) 258–61.

[54] Judith Plaskow, *Standing Again at Sinai: Judaism from a Feminist Perspective* (San Francisco: Harper & Row, 1990) xv, 105. She sees such inclusive communities as necessary for the recovery of the fullness of Torah. "The creation of Jewish communities in which differences are valued as necessary parts of a greater whole is the institutional and experiential foundation for the recovery of the fullness of Torah" (106).

[55] Ibid., 13–15, drawing on the hermeneutical work of Elisabeth Schüssler Fiorenza, *Bread Not Stone: The Challenge of Feminist Biblical Interpretation* (Boston: Beacon Press, 1984). See more recently Elisabeth Schüssler Fiorenza, *Rhetoric and Ethic: The Politics of Biblical Studies* (Minneapolis: Fortress Press, 1999), reviewed by Carolyn Osiek in *Theological Studies* 61 (September 2000) 553–5 and by Karen A. Barta, *Theological Studies* 61 (December 2000) 750–2. Sandra M. Schneiders, *Written That You May Believe: Encountering Jesus in the Fourth Gospel* (New York: Crossroad, 1999) 129, also drawing on the work of Schüssler Fiorenza, comments: "Because the biblical text itself is not purely and simply a text of liberation for women but is itself part of the problem, the transformational hermeneutic of feminism aims not only at the liberation of the oppressed through the transformation of society (the aim of all liberationist theology and interpretation) but at the liberation of the biblical text from its own participation in the oppression of women and the transformation of the church that continues to model, underwrite, and legitimate the oppression of women in family and society." For an excellent systematic work on the whole question of hermeneutics, see Sandra M. Schneiders, *The Revelatory Text: Interpreting the New Testament as Sacred Scripture,* 2d ed. (Collegeville: The Liturgical Press, 1999).

[56] Plaskow, *Standing Again at Sinai,* 53.

[57] Ibid., 56.

[58] Frederick Herzog, *God-Walk: Liberation Shaping Dogmatics* (Maryknoll, N.Y.: Orbis Books, 1988) xxii, cited three times in Rieger, *Remember the Poor,* 4, 123, 226.

[59] Frederick Herzog, *Justice Church: The New Function of the Church in North American Christianity* (Maryknoll, N.Y.: Orbis Books, 1980) 39. Chapter 2 (30–54) is entitled "Jesus and Power."

[60] Ibid., 43–4. He refers to the "ethnic dilemma" of Christianity: Christian identity in Jesus means Christian identity in the corporate selfhood of Israel.

[61] Rieger, *Remember the Poor,* 219. Plaskow, *Standing Again at Sinai,* refers frequently to her experiences with women's groups and especially to B'not Esh, "an ongoing Jewish feminist spirituality collective . . . a community of vision and struggle" (xii, 212, 234).

[62] Terry A. Veling, *Living in the Margins: Intentional Communities and the Art of Interpretation* (New York: Crossroad, 1996) 17. His book offers a very fine review of various approaches to hermeneutics under the rubrics of "dialogical hermeneutics" (engaging the book from "inside"), "exilic hermeneutics" (risking the book from "outside"), and "marginal hermeneutics" (rewriting the book from "in-between"). The latter reveals the tension within religious traditions "generated by two interplaying needs: the need for identity, continuity, guiding norms, and the need for new understanding, relevance, and responsiveness to changing situations" (187). See my review in *Theological Studies* 58 (June 1997) 396–7.

[63] Rieger, *Remember the Poor,* 161, commenting on Gustavo Gutiérrez's view of the oppression of women, observes: "As soon as those who are repressed make their presence felt, the powers that be react with further acts of repression." This applies equally well to the history of Christianity in its awareness and treatment of the Jews.

[64] Boys, *Has God Only One Blessing?* 10–11. The purpose of her book is to bring recent scholarship about Jewish-Christian relations into the consciousness and practice of those pastoral agents responsible for Christian education on its various levels.

[65] George M. Smiga, *Pain and Polemic: Anti-Judaism in the Gospels* (Mahwah, N.J.: Paulist Press, 1992) 11–23. For Douglas Hare's threefold classification see his "The Rejection of the Jews in the Synoptic Gospels and Acts," *Anti-Semitism and the Foundations of Christianity,* ed. Alan Davies (Mahwah, N.J.: Paulist Press, 1979) 27–47. For the distinction on the types of Jewish-Gentile Christianity see Raymond E. Brown, "Not Jewish Christianity and Gentile Christianity, but Types of Jewish/Gentile Christianity," *Catholic Biblical Quarterly* 45 (1983) 74–9; also in Raymond E. Brown and John P. Meier, *Antioch and Rome: New Testament Cradles of Catholic Christianity* (Mahwah, N.J.: Paulist Press, 1983), employed in the form of a chart by Boys, *Has God Only One Blessing?* 145–7. Smiga expresses the distinction between prophetic and subordinating polemic as follows: "In prophetic polemic, Jewish groups are criticized for a failure to live up to the terms of the covenant which they themselves profess to accept. In subordinating polemic, Jewish groups are criticized for failing to accept what they would see as a redefinition of that covenant" (20). James D. G. Dunn offers a fine discussion of the issues in his essay "The Question of Anti-Semitism in the New Testament Writings of the Period," *Jews and Christians,* ed. Dunn, 177–211.

[66] Jon D. Levenson, *The Death and Resurrection of the Beloved Son: The Transformation of Child Sacrifice in Judaism and Christianity* (New Haven, Conn.: Yale University Press, 1993) 70. In citing a rabbinic midrash (*Sifre Deut.* 312) that has parallels to the parable of the wicked husbandmen (Mark 12:1-12 par.), he comments further: "The biblical texts on which the two contending groups focused are, in each case, those that speak of the origins of the faithful community and the legitimation of its separation from its unworthy competitor, and, in each case, the legitimation derives from God's new and definitive act of election" (231). He concludes that the relationship between Judaism and Christianity is best characterized "as a rivalry of two siblings for their father's unique blessing" (232). See also Jon D. Levenson, "Is There a Counterpart in the Hebrew Bible to New Testament

Anti-Semitism?" *Journal of Ecumenical Studies* 22 (Spring 1985) 242–60. His point in this article is "that the material in the Hebrew Bible which touches on non-Israelite *religion,* like the material in the New Testament which touches on Judaism, is born in the white heat of polemic. In both cases, the sarcastic, reductionistic literature of polemic has come to be regarded as sacred Scripture" (254–5, emphasis in original). Luke T. Johnson, "The New Testament's Anti-Jewish Slander and the Conventions of Ancient Polemic," *Journal of Biblical Literature* 108 (1989) 419–41, gives numerous citations from Greek, Roman, and Jewish literature to show that what we consider harsh and indeed slanderous language was a widespread phenomenon in ancient polemic. It was normal to refer to one's opponents as hypocrites, blind guides, possessed by demons, etc. "I suggest that the slander of the NT is typical of that found among rival claimants to a philosophical tradition and is found as widely among Jews as among other Hellenists. I further suggest that the way the NT talks about Jews is just about the way all opponents talked about each other back then" (429).

[67] This is one of John Pawlikowski's final suggestions in *What Are They Saying About Christian-Jewish Relations,* 144–5. For a call to interreligious dialogue among Muslims, Christians, and Jews around the theme of messianism, see Riffat Hassan, "Messianism and Islam," *Journal of Ecumenical Studies* 22 (Spring 1985) 261–91.

[68] Paul D. Hanson, *The People Called: The Growth of Community in the Bible* (San Francisco: Harper & Row, 1986) 477.

[69] Neusner, *Rabbinic Judaism,* 165. See the whole of chapter 7, "Ethnos: Israel's Teleology—the Messiah," 144–65.

[70] Pinchas Lapide and Ulrich Luz, *Jesus in Two Perspectives: A Jewish-Christian Dialog,* trans. Lawrence W. Denef (Minneapolis: Augsburg, 1985) 54.

[71] Ibid., 118–9. The citation is from H.-W. Bartsch, "Umkehr zu Israel," *Evangelische Zeitstimmen* 22/23 (1965) 7ff.

[72] Rosemary Ruether sees the key issue that divides Christians and Jews to be Christology. "Is it possible to say, 'Jesus is Messiah' without, implicitly or explicitly, saying at the same time 'and the Jews be damned'?" Ruether, *Faith and Fratricide,* 246. Gregory Baum, in his introduction to the same volume, says that Ruether calls the Christian rejection of the Jewish interpretation of the Scriptures and its consequent anti-Semitism "the left hand of Christology" (ibid., 12). James D. G. Dunn refers to this in *Jews and Christians,* 178, but in his conclusions says that the focus on Christology may be anachronistic for the early centuries. "In the late first century and early second century the question was much more *theo*logical, as the issue of how the one God had most clearly revealed his will and effected his saving purpose. And that was still a debate about relativities (Christ more than Torah) than of complete and mutually exclusive opposites" (211, emphasis in original).

CHAPTER TWO

"Where Is the God of Justice?" (Mal 2:17)

The Blessing of Jacob-Israel

"Now therefore, if you obey my voice and keep my covenant, you shall be my treasured possession *[sĕgūllâ]* out of all the peoples" (Exod 19:5). When Israel faces its creator, it is unique, set apart as a holy people consecrated to the service of God: "You shall be holy, for I the LORD your God am holy" (Lev 19:2b). "Put simply: only Israel, the Jewish people, has Israel's relationship with God."[1] This is an important insight to be kept clearly in mind. Other people may have a relationship with Israel's God, but only Israel has *Israel's* relationship to God. In this sense, Israel is destined to be "other." For Christians, this creates what Frederick Herzog has called an "ethnic dilemma" insofar as Christian identity in *Jesus* means in some sense Christian identity in the corporate selfhood of Israel. Whatever one's position on whether there are two covenants or one covenant,[2] Jesus himself in his historical life and mission was thoroughly Jewish in the best sense of being deeply committed to the heritage of Israel, not the least of which is the recognition that Israel is not only chosen by God, but chosen precisely to be "a covenant to the people, a light to the nations" (Isa 42:6).[3] To understand the biblical notion of justice, then, we must attend to Israel's relationship to YHWH, particularly in terms of covenantal fidelity, and to Israel's relationship to other peoples (or nations) in terms of that same fidelity.[4]

Methodologically, we will focus upon our "common root," primarily the Hebrew Bible, while recognizing the diverse traditions of its interpretation. To do this in an even remotely adequate way would require the kind of dialogue that Michael Signer proposes.[5] This chapter does not pretend to achieve that goal. Rather, it offers a line of interpretation around the theme of justice that strives to remain sensitive to the traditions of both Jews and Christians. In the light of the preceding chapter, it must be remembered that the primary aim of rabbinic exegesis is to perpetuate a levitical system around the *sefer* Torah. Therefore, the principal though not exclusive focus is upon the five books of Moses, i.e., the unity and divinity of the Torah of Moses, as source and ground of fulfilling the very *practical* requirements of Deuteronomy 10:12-13 to fear (reverence) YHWH, to walk in all his ways, to love him, to serve him with all one's heart and soul, and to keep all his commandments and decrees as Moses has given them to Israel for the good of the people.

While there have been and are "competing Judaic religious systems," as Jacob Neusner has pointed out, still they must all measure themselves in relation to the enduring system of rabbinic Judaism as articulated in Mishnah and Talmud (just as Christian interpreters must measure themselves in relation to the enduring orthodoxy of the first seven ecumenical councils formulated during the patristic period from 325 to 787). The instinctual centering upon the person of Moses or, perhaps better, on Moses' personal experience of YHWH as the foundational religious experience of Israel, cannot be ignored or set aside. However one interprets the Torah as given to Moses on Mount Sinai, one cannot ignore or deny the reality and experience of Moses without destroying the Jewish religion (just as one cannot ignore or deny the reality and experience of Jesus without destroying the Christian religion). Both Moses and Jesus are foundational and indispensable to all subsequent traditions of interpretation in each religion. Martin Buber, for example, in his fine book on Moses which does engage the critical studies of the time, advocates a reading of the text of Exodus as saga that communicates historical reality; in other words, while one may differentiate legendary accretions and later developments, there still lies at the core the figure of Moses and his experience as the essential root of all subsequent history and reflection. This is not quite the same as saying that everything was given with Moses, but it is saying that without Moses nothing was given. In a very real sense, everything is contained in the experience of Moses at "Horeb, the mountain of God" (Exod 3:1) where YHWH reveals his name for all generations (Exod 3:13-15).[6]

It must also be remembered that the primary aim of Christian exegesis (especially among the authors of the "New Testament") is to demonstrate from the Hebrew Scriptures and in the light of the death and resurrection of Jesus prophetic fulfillment of Israel's hopes. In a sense, everything is contained in the revelation of Jesus' resurrection, which, of course, cannot be understood apart from Jesus' historical life and death that precede and the ongoing life of the Church that follows and is born out of that revelation. But neither can it be understood apart from the history of Israel as contained in the Hebrew Bible—our common root which precedes both traditions and is largely foreign to them.[7] There is a value to engaging the covenantal claims of the two traditions at this level of explicit theological affirmation as Signer proposes,[8] but our purpose is somewhat distinct. Taking our cue from Jon Levenson, we must find ways to allow historical criticism to interact with these other senses of Scripture. In the present chapter, we will follow the rabbinic rule of putting primary emphasis on the first five books of Moses as revealing the Hebrew sense of justice while using the prophetic books (Joshua to Malachi) as a form of commentary. This will yield a sense that justice, to be effective, must take structural or institutional form. Then, in the next chapter, we will propose that such structural justice is precisely what Jesus, still within the traditions of his ancestors, was trying to create in his own day. This may seem to leave out the Christian side of the equation, but it is the hope that such a viewpoint will renew the Christian view, affirm what is deepest and best in the Jewish view, and move the dialogue to a different level of engagement.

Since we will be relying on the methods of modern hermeneutics, a further word needs to be said about the approach taken here. We have already noted the need to relate the historical-critical (diachronic) method and the canonical/literary (synchronic) method. Exegetes may choose one or the other for specific purposes, but both are necessary for a full treatment of the text.[9] An adequate hermeneutical theory will recognize that there is a "world behind the text" (the sociohistorical context), a "world of the text" (the literary/canonical reality of the text itself), and a "world before the text" (the effective history, i.e., reading and reception of the text in subsequent generations to the present).[10] This, of course, raises complex issues and not everything can be said at once. Insofar as we will focus on the Pentateuch, mention must be made of the documentary hypothesis which is much under discussion today. The classic distinction in authorship is made between "J" (Yahwist), "E" (Elohist), "P" (Priestly), "D" (Deuteronomy), as well as "R" (a final Redactor) who has variously been thought to be of the "P" or of the "D/Dtr" (deuteronomic history that includes Joshua to 2 Kings) or, more rarely, of the "J" school or tendency.[11] These distinctions are useful for sorting out various theological tendencies and thus not reducing everything to a *single* biblical theology. With the rabbinic tradition, it is important to recognize diversity of viewpoint, the possibility of debate because of texts that seem to contradict or be in conflict with each other, so that not everything is immediately resolvable. As an example from a Christian exegete, Norbert Lohfink differentiates the deuteronomic stratum of the Pentateuch, with its "perfectly ruthless theology of war," from the priestly stratum (more precisely, the priestly historical narrative designated "p^g") that simply "eliminated war from the story it tells."[12] The point is that such distinctions are useful for recognizing diverse theological tendencies. At the same time, we will be primarily concerned with reflection upon the canonical redaction of the whole Hebrew Bible in the form of the Tanakh (the Masoretic text of the rabbinic tradition) because this, in some form, was the tradition that Jesus knew.[13]

The question of this chapter, given Israel's uniqueness, is what constitutes Israel as Israel. The answer, put thematically and to be developed in the rest of the chapter, is the Exodus experience as liberation from exile (serving Pharaoh) for a renewed life serving YHWH, the God of their fathers, in "a land flowing with milk and honey" (Exod 3:7-12). Although many scholars separate the Exodus, the giving of Torah, and the conquest, we are treating the Exodus-conquest as literarily a single story, as do the post-exilic editors of the Pentateuch and many of the psalms (e.g., Psalms 78; 105; 106; 114; 135; 136). For the sake of clarity, however, this will be developed in three steps: (1) liberation from exile: the origins of Israel in Egypt and Canaan and its corresponding self-understanding as a people set apart; (2) a renewed life serving the God of their fathers: the centrality and importance of the covenant and the corresponding embodiment of that relationship in terms of YHWH's *mišpāṭ* and *ṣĕdāqâ* (the crucial question of God's justice); (3) "a land flowing with milk and honey": Israel's destiny as realizing YHWH's *šālôm* (the priestly ideal of return to God's original intention at creation) in the land that belongs to YHWH alone.[14]

Liberation from Exile: The Origins of Israel

"You shall not oppress a resident alien *[gēr]*; you know the heart of an alien, for you were aliens in the land of Egypt" (Exod 23:9). In the entire Covenant Code (Exod 20:22–23:33), there are only two instructions that indicate an immediate and personal response on the part of YHWH. First: "You shall not abuse any widow or orphan. If you do abuse them, when they cry out to me, I will surely heed their cry; my wrath will burn, and I will kill you with the sword, and your wives shall become widows and your children orphans" (Exod 22:22-24). And second: "If you take your neighbor's cloak in pawn, you shall restore it before the sun goes down; for it may be your neighbor's only clothing to use as a cover; in what else shall that person sleep? And if your neighbor cries out to me, I will listen, for I am compassionate" (Exod 22:26-27). The verse in between (22:25) draws a parallel between "my people" *[ʿammî]* and "the poor *[ʿanî]* among you." Exodus 22:21-27 along with 23:1-9 express the concerns of legal justice for the weak and powerless: the resident alien, the widow, the orphan, the poor, especially those who are in debt and are oppressed by the lack of justice in the courts. "You shall not pervert the justice due to your poor *[mišpāṭ ʾebyōnkā]* in their lawsuits" (Exod 23:6). YHWH is their protector as he protected the poor and powerless in the land of Egypt.

There is much discussion today about the historical origins of the people of Israel.[15] Whatever theory or model one employs to combine the phenomena into a coherent scenario, there seem to be three historical elements that underlie the narrative as we have it in the Hebrew Bible: (1) The phenomenon known as *ʿapīru* (probably not related to the biblical term *ʿibrî* or "Hebrew" as a term of distinctive identity in relation to foreigners, e.g., at Exod 1:15-22; cp. Gen 10:21; 39:15, 17; 40:15). These are groups that do not accept the established order of the king or ruler in the city-state and so become outlaws and mercenaries who withdraw from the cities, usually into the highlands (although the withdrawal might simply mean refusal of allegiance to the ruling powers). (2) The presence in Canaan of Israel in some form before the Exodus; in other words, of a group that worshiped the god *ʾel* rather than *baʿal,* probably as *ʿapīru* who withdrew from the oppression of the city-state and found in *ʾel* a god of compassion. They had a tribal style of life in the villages of the highlands and/or as nomadic shepherds. (3) The entrance into Canaan of a different group of *ʿapīru* from the south who proclaim the victory of YHWH in Egypt (Exod 15:20-21; cp. Deut 33:2; Judg 5:4 where YHWH is said to have come from Sinai, Seir [Edom], and Mount Paran). This group is the most difficult to reconstruct historically, yet paradoxically, it is the center of the biblical story. At some point, "the story of deliverance from Pharaoh" by YHWH "became the story of deliverance from the power of the Canaanite kings."[16] And YHWH from the south became one with *ʾel* in the highlands of Canaan.

As a minimum, the emergence of Israel is now seen "as a complex phenomenon involving, first, the arrival of new peoples in the central hills from a variety of sources, including especially the collapsing cities of the Egypto-Canaanite empire, and, second, the gradual process of ethnic self-identification that generated an elaborate genealogy linking the highlanders to each other."[17] While modern scholars tend to focus on the highlanders in Canaan, the biblical story focuses on that strange group of *ʿapīru* who arrived from the south under the leadership of a religious genius named Moses. His experience of this god who calls himself *ʾehyeh* (Exod 3:12: "I will be with you"; 3:14: "I will be what [or who] I will be" and "I will be sent me to you") is inseparably connected to "the God of your fathers" (3:6 in the singular and 3:13 in the plural), "the God of Abraham, the God of Isaac, and the God of Jacob."[18] For our purposes it is not necessary to review the entire history of the origins of Israel from Abraham to Moses but simply to ask with the rabbinic tradition: what truly makes Israel free? What counts as liberation from exile? Exile refers to both God's creation bound by sin (Genesis 1–11) and God's people, the children of Jacob, bound by slavery at the hands of despotic kings (Exodus 1; 2:23-25). The answer in the rabbinic tradition focuses upon the binding of Isaac (the *aqedah:* Gen 22:1-19) and the protection of Israel as YHWH's "firstborn son" (the *pešaḥ:* Exod 4:22; 12:11-13, 21-27). In the tradition of rabbinic midrash, according to Jon Levenson, what YHWH "sees" (Exod 12:13 connected to Gen 22:8, 14 and 1 Chr 21:15) is the blood of Isaac: "And, once again, whether the son's blood was thought to have been literally shed or not, it is this blood that God sees when he renounces punishment and spares Israel from devastation. The *aqedah*/passover sacrifice has become the efficient cause of Israel's rescue from affliction throughout history."[19]

The beginning of that rescue and freedom is then the story of Abraham. It is the story of God's initiative (Gen 12:1-3) and Abraham's response of absolute obedience to the voice of YHWH (Gen 12:4). Abraham did not simply believe that the word of YHWH (the blessing and promise of descendants) was true; he entrusted himself to YHWH (Gen 15:6a: *wĕhe ʾĕmin baYHWH*).[20] The rest of Genesis 15:6 is translated: "and the LORD reckoned it to him as righteousness" (NRSV) or "He reckoned it to his merit" (NJPS). In Hebrew the subject of the second verb could continue to be Abraham, so that it is Abraham who reckoned to YHWH *ṣĕdāqâ*. Both versions are true, for it is the initiative of YHWH, the authority of his word, which Abraham embraces with complete and absolute trust, that creates the possibility of *ṣĕdāqâ* in Abraham and hence for all subsequent generations. The rabbinic tradition encapsulates this in the word *zekhut,* which refers to the "unearned grace" that enables Israel to fulfill God's justice *(mišpāṭ)* and so is also called merit.

> The principal message of the story of the beginnings, as sages read Genesis, is that the world depends upon the *zekhut* of Abraham, Isaac, and Jacob; Israel, for its part, enjoys access to that *zekhut,* being today the family of the patriarchs and matriarchs. That conception of matters constitutes the sages' doctrine of history: the family forms the basic and irreducible historical unit. Israel is not so much a nation as a family, and the heritage of the patriarchs and matriarchs sustains that family from the beginning even to the end. So the sages' doctrine of history transforms history into genealogy.[21]

The *zekhut* of Abraham flows from the binding of Isaac, as Neusner notes, but what makes this story poignant is that Abraham, Sarah, and Isaac are YHWH's own family, and now YHWH is invoking his absolute claim upon the firstborn son.

> The aptness of the incident derives from its domestic character: relationship of mother, father, and only child. What Abraham and Isaac were prepared to sacrifice (and Sarah to lose) won for them and their descendants—as the story itself makes explicit—an ongoing treasury of *zekhut*. So the children of Abraham and Isaac through history will derive salvation from the original act of binding Isaac to the altar.[22]

This is true, but what gives the story its deepest meaning is chosenness. YHWH always chooses carefully and well (the grace of election) those who by their trials fulfill his *ṣĕdāqâ*.

> The larger theological point is that the trials of the righteous serve to demonstrate not God's injustice, as many think to be the case, but quite the opposite, the fairness of his choices. For those choices are not mere whims, evidence of the arbitrariness of providence, and the proof is that those chosen, like Abraham, for exaltation, are able to pass the brutal tests to which God subjects them and thus to vindicate the grace he has shown them. . . . The trials of the righteous mediate the contradiction between God's grace and his justice.[23]

As Levenson shows so well, whatever the etiological significance of the *aqedah* in later interpretations, especially in regard to child sacrifice, the point of the story is Abraham's absolute and unquestioning surrender to God's intentions. At Genesis 18:16-33, Abraham questions God in the sense of challenging God to be consistent with the divine character and intention: "Shall not the judge of all the earth do what is just?" (Gen 18:25: *lōʿ yaʿăśeh mišpāṭ*). Indeed, YHWH includes Abraham in his plans because he has chosen Abraham to instruct future generations "to keep the way of the LORD by doing righteousness and justice" (Gen 18:19). But, in the case of Isaac, there is no other plan or intention than Isaac himself. He is the promise and as the firstborn he belongs wholly to God. The rabbinic tradition often includes Isaac's acceptance of his sacrificial role,[24] but the focus of the story is on Abraham's fear (reverence) of God: "Do not lay your hand on the boy or do anything to him; for now I know that you fear God, since you have not withheld your son, your only son, from me" (Gen 22:12). This is repeated in verses 15-18 with the promise of the blessings of offspring and land, as well as the blessing for the nations, "because you have obeyed my voice." Thus, God's grace, God's initiative, calls for a human response of trust and obedience. It is not merely a matter of trust but a giving of oneself that takes concrete and specific shape in obedience. It demands "strength of character and self-knowledge."[25] From Abraham's *zekhut* flows salvation for "YHWH will see" the blood of Isaac, i.e., Abraham's reverential obedience, as grace that became effective (merit) for all future generations. This is what makes Israel free.

In the story of the Exodus, we see the same process at work. As Levenson has emphasized, Israel's freedom in the Exodus experience lies in its complete and inescapable subjugation to YHWH. In a strong critique of many liberationist views, he affirms what must never be forgotten, that Israel is a "kin-group":

> Throughout the Hebrew Bible, Israel is portrayed as a natural family, a kin-group and not a voluntary association, a mystical sodality, or, as these liberationists would have it, a socioeconomic class or political movement. It is not incidental that the book of Exodus begins with a genealogy; the preferential option for the poor and the chosenness of Israel are not to be *equated* and, though both can be heard in the story of the exodus, it is the chosenness of Israel that dominates there.[26]

This kinship originates in God's feelings for Israel. The opening of the account of God's initiative in the Exodus (Exod 2:23-25) describes God with four verbs that indicate a very personal and passionate involvement: God "heard" (their groaning under their slavery *[ʿbd]*); God "remembered" (his covenant with Abraham, Isaac, and Jacob [the root *zkr* may echo the later rabbinic notion of *zekhut*]); God "saw" (the sons of Israel [the root *yrʿ* recalls the *aqedah*]); and God "knew" (no object [*ydʿ* evokes the kind of intimate, personal knowledge that Adam had when he "knew" his wife Eve]).

YHWH's deep feeling for the people is predicated on the fact that Israel is his "firstborn son" (Exod 4:22), chosen to be a people set apart, God's own treasured possession out of all the peoples, but first God had to bear them away "on eagles' wings" (Exod 19:4-6; Deut 32:7-14) in order to teach them how to fly.[27] The first step toward liberation, then, is deliverance from the situation of oppression, i.e., bondage, slavery, destitution, in which they find themselves by reason of imperial power. Here is where the preferential option for the poor makes sense. Norbert Lohfink sees the Exodus story as the "prototype of God's concern for the poor."[28] He cites Deuteronomy 26:5-10 as a credo that makes "deliverance from poverty" its main theme (vv. 6-7) and then outlines six steps that underlie this later confession of faith. First, YHWH takes "a nation for himself from the midst of another nation" (Deut 4:34), i.e., "the whole exploited lower class of Egypt," which would have been a large group within the total population (see the comments on the *ʿapīru* above). Second, as reflected in the first and fifth chapters of Exodus, as well as Deuteronomy 26:5-10, the poverty of the people is "system-related," i.e., the result of deliberate human choices that has become systemic as "economic exploitation and social degradation." Third, the decisive step involves a change in societal structures:

> Yahweh's intervention does not aim, as do such acts of assistance elsewhere in the ancient Near East, to lighten the suffering while leaving the system intact or perhaps even aiding its renewed stabilization. Instead, the poor are removed from the impoverishing situation. Nowhere else in the ancient Near East have I encountered in the context of divine aid to the poor even the remotest suggestion that a god might physically remove the poor who cry to him or her from the world that oppresses them as human beings.[29]

Lohfink reviews the narrative in Exodus to demonstrate that attempts to aid the people other than removal were tried but were ineffective. The daughter of Pharaoh does an individual act of charity (2:1-10), but it has no effect on the rest of the people. Moses' act of "counter-terror" (2:11-15) only produces fear in the oppressed but no change. The "reformist" attempts of Moses and Aaron (5:1-23) only intensify the oppression. The plagues (7:1–11:10) represent "the inevitable catastrophe of an unjust system," but paradoxically prepare for the alternative. This leads to the fourth step: "A deed like this is impossible for human beings. In the Exodus, the removal of the poor from the system that enslaves them is the work of Yahweh alone."[30] Thus, fifth, the Exodus is a miracle of the creativity of God, who conquers chaos (symbolized by the sea at Exodus 14) and creates a new order, a new society embodied in the promise of "a land flowing with milk and honey," i.e., a new order as intended by God from the beginning of creation and established at Sinai as "a new society that knows no more poverty" as seen in the book of Deuteronomy (e.g., Deut 6:20-25):

> According to this order, Yahweh intends that Israel be a nation of sisters and brothers in which there will be no more poor (cf. Deut 15:4). This in itself makes clear that, according to the Bible, the poor of Egypt are to become, through the Exodus, a kind of divinely-willed contrast-society.[31]

This image of Israel as a "contrast-society" is his sixth and final step. It opens the way to our next section on the centrality and importance of the covenant as embodying YHWH's *mišpāṭ*. At Deuteronomy 4:5-8 Moses teaches "statutes" *(ḥuqqîm)* and "ordinances" *(mišpāṭîm)* which, if they are observed, will reveal Israel as "a wise and discerning people" among the nations. Two things characterize this people: no other nation has a god so near to it as YHWH (v. 7) and no other nation has statutes and ordinances as just *(ṣaddîqîm)* as is contained in all this *tôrâ* (v. 8).

Election and deliverance from exile now mean that the people must learn how to fly in a way that is unique and distinctive to them as YHWH's chosen.

A New Life with God: Covenantal Fidelity and Justice

Underlying all the covenantal formulations, whether in the form of a "grant" or of a "treaty," underlying all the statutes and ordinances and teaching *(tôrâ)*, is the simple statement "I will be your God and you will be my people" (Exod 6:4, 7 [cf. 3:7-12]; Deut 26:16-19; Hos 2:23; Jer 7:23; 30:22; 31:1, 33; Ezek 36:28; Zech 8:8), and even more to the point, in various formulations, "I will be your father and you will be my son" (Exod 4:22; Deut 1:31; 14:1-2 [children and people in parallel]; 32:6; 2 Sam 7:14 [said of the son of David]; Hos 11:1-4, 8; Jer 3:4, 19; 31:9, 20; Isa 43:1-7; 63:16; 64:8; Mal 1:6; 2:10; Pss 2:7; 89:26-27 [royal Psalms of David]). In the rabbinic tradition, God's merciful love *(ḥesed)* is greater than his justice *(mišpāṭ)*.[32] Frank Moore Cross affirms, "*ḥesed* is a kinship term." It assumes along with other familial terms mutual obligations and privileges on the part of the "Divine Kinsman" and on the part of "the family of the deity." But the movement is from "the language of kinship, kinship-in-flesh" (the language of "brotherhood" and "fatherhood," of "love" and "loyalty") to "the language of covenant: kinship-in-law." Failure to recognize that the term covenant *(bĕrît)* is rooted in societies organized around kinship has led to distortions such as the arbitrary separation of covenants of "grant" (or divine grace) and covenants of "treaty" (or mutual obligation) which fails to recognize that *all* covenants involve mutual bonding.[33]

Within the familial paradigm, no vision of such bonding is more dramatic and inclusive of all the themes that constitute this relationship than Hosea 2:16-20, which had influence upon the deuteronomic tradition (D/Dtr). Within the image of a marriage covenant, the prophet speaks of an eternal and universal covenant of peace in the spousal bond of righteousness *(bĕṣedeq)* and justice *(bĕmišpāṭ)*, of steadfast love *(bĕḥesed)* and compassion *(bĕraḥămîm)*, of faithfulness *(bĕ ʾĕmûnâ)* so that "you will know the LORD" *(bĕyādaʿat ʾet-YHWH)*.

To understand the notion of justice in the Hebrew Bible, we must see it very concretely as including all these covenantal virtues and as oriented to the final peace *(šālôm)* that only God can give. At root, justice is "fidelity to the demands of a relationship."[34] We turn now to the idea of covenant as a personal relationship of fidelity or loyalty and then to the compelling insistence upon justice as the *only way* to guarantee that such love and service will be effective.

This consideration of covenant is organized around five statements: (1) the story of YHWH's "loyalty" to his people is the context that makes the whole intelligible; (2) there is only one covenant theologically, that given to Moses on Sinai; (3) the covenant is always being renewed, so that talk of a "new covenant" (Jer 31:31) must be understood dialectically; (4) the corresponding "loyalty" of the people demands the fulfillment of all the commands, statutes, and ordinances, both ethical and ritual; (5) the "distinctiveness" of Israel's covenant is moral response and commitment, so that justice is always at the center of what it means to be God's people.

First, the story of YHWH's loyalty. Katharine Doob Sakenfeld translates *ḥesed* as "loyalty." Drawing upon "stories of human loyalty" in the Hebrew Bible, she affirms three irreducible elements in the term *ḥesed:* commitment in a relationship that manifests itself in concrete action, the critical need of the recipient that puts the recipient in a position of dependence, and the freedom of the one who shows loyalty in the sense that there are no societal legal sanctions for failure to show loyalty. She summarizes its application to God's covenant loyalty:

> God's relationship to Israel was expressed in the Old Testament primarily under a covenant metaphor. Divine loyalty within covenant involved both God's commitment to Israel and the ever new free decision of God to continue to honor that commitment by preserving and supporting the covenant community. Divine freedom and divine self-obligation were held together in this single word, which expressed also God's strength and Israel's need for divine care.[35]

God's commitment and ever new free decision is, of course, the unfolding story of a promised future in which the people's history and experience is surrounded by the presence of God. "I will be with you." The people come to know who God is, a God of "abounding loyalty" (*rab-ḥesed* at Exod 34:6)[36] as he walks with them on the way. The story is the ethic, as Janzen says, and gives context and meaning to the relationship between YHWH and the people, but the fulfillment of that relationship as narrated is the covenantal instruction *(tôrâ)*.

"The covenant without stipulations, the Abrahamic covenant of Genesis 15 and 17, is only a preparation for the Sinaitic covenant, into which it is absorbed."[37] Our second point is that, theologically, there is only one covenant, the completion of Israel's election at Sinai as recorded at Exodus 24:3-8 and renewed at Exodus 34:10. As Ernest Nicholson points out in his fine book on the covenant, the Hebrew Bible describes more than one occasion of a covenant between YHWH and Israel: Deuteronomy 29:1 (in the land of Moab), Joshua 24:25ff. (at Schechem), 2 Kings 23:3 (Josiah), as well as Exodus 19–24 and 34:10-27 (although Deuteronomy 4–5 and 9:7–10:5 ignore the latter in favor of one covenant at Sinai).

> Theologically we touch here upon an understanding of the relationship between Yahweh and Israel which was one of the distinctive

> contributions of the notion of a covenant between them to Old Testament faith: that Israel's status as Yahweh's people was not something grounded in the nature of things, something divinely guaranteed as permanent as though inherent in a fixed cosmic order, but rather that it was constituted by Yahweh's decision and choice and no less by Israel's.[38]

This confirms once again that the covenant idea, theologically, always involves a relationship of mutual obligation between YHWH and Israel, YHWH's choice of Israel and Israel's response.

To see the theological center of the idea of covenant at Sinai is not to deny that the term is analogous and is used in various ways. Lohfink speaks of many "covenant theologies" in the field of Scripture study and observes that the "deuteronomistic" view is not immediately compatible with the "priestly."

> In the one case its meaning is something like a contract which can be broken and then is at an end (this is the original deuteronomistic notion); in the other, its meaning is rather a solemn promise made by God under oath which an unfaithful partner cannot simply destroy by his or her infidelity (this is the original priestly notion). The Hebrew word behind all this, *berît,* can make both statements. It is the context that determines which of the two possibilities is meant. Further, the priestly presentation of history, with the two great promises to the whole human race (in the post-diluvial ancestor, Noah) and to the chosen people (in the ancestor, Abraham), has deliberately suppressed from its historical plan the somewhat older notion of a contract-like covenant between God and the people of Israel on Mount Sinai.[39]

However one resolves the tensions and apparent inconsistencies, not to mention changes, in the historical development schematized as creation, exodus, and eschaton, it must be emphasized with Jon Levenson that the Sinaitic covenant dominates the Hebrew Bible (e.g., the block from Exodus 19 to the close of 2 Kings), while the Davidic covenant is expounded with clarity and detail only at 2 Samuel 7 and Psalm 89. Moreover, even more forcefully, Israel was a people with its laws from Moses before it was ever a state with its own king (David), and it survived the destruction of the state without loss of that essential identity conferred at Sinai.[40] However interpreted historically, this is the crucial *theological* point. Indeed, in the rabbinic tradition, the *tôrâ* of Moses has enabled the people of Israel to maintain their identity in the face of the loss of state, Temple, and even land! And still, the identity of the people at Sinai is indelibly rooted in the *zekhut* of Abraham. The *aqedah* and the *pešaḥ* are inseparably linked in the constitution of Israel.

This brings us to our third statement, that the covenant is always being renewed. Of course, whenever the people celebrate *pešaḥ* they are not just remembering a past event but experiencing that event as a living reality in the present (Deut 5:1-3; 6:4-9). Levenson makes this point by connecting the celebration of covenant renewal (e.g., Psalms 50; 81) on Zion with Sinai. "In short, the renewal of the Sinaitic covenant has become a liturgy of the Temple of Jerusalem. . . . The voice of Sinai is heard on Zion."[41] Correspondingly, when Jeremiah (31:31-34) speaks of "a new covenant," he does not contrast it with an "old" covenant, but with Israel's "brokenness" at the time of the exile (587 B.C.E.). He emphasizes that this is a new covenant "with the house of Israel and the house of Judah" so that now God's *tôrâ* (which continues) will be a matter of the heart, of the full realization of what underlies the whole covenantal experience of Israel: "I will be their God and they shall be my people" (v. 33c). What is entailed is deep personal knowledge of YHWH based in God's greatest sign of loyalty, the divine forgiveness.[42] Jeremiah 31:31-34 must be read within the larger context of Jeremiah 30:1– 31:40, which emphasizes the return from exile with the promise of the land that YHWH gave to their ancestors (30:3; 31:27). Thus, there is a dialectical continuity in that the earlier covenant continues; it is the *same* covenant, but now is different, as transformed by the divine creativity and loyalty. "Despite all the rhetorical counterpoint, what lies hidden in the Jeremiah text is not the rationale of the completely different, utterly outmoded earlier one, the purer antithesis, but the fuller and more lasting actualization of what was given of old."[43] This should hold true for all Christian talk of "covenant," and it surely held true for Jesus, for God's love for Israel is everlasting and faithful: "Thus says the LORD: The people who survived the sword found grace in the wilderness [Exod 33:12-17]; when Israel sought for rest, the LORD appeared to him [Moses] long ago. I have loved you with an everlasting love; therefore I have continued my faithfulness *[ḥesed]* to you" (Jer 31:2-3).

YHWH's faithful love or loyalty calls for a response of loyalty on the part of the people. This corresponding loyalty demands the fulfillment of all the commands *(miṣbôt)*, statutes *(ḥuqqîm)*, and ordinances *(mišpāṭîm)* as given in the teaching/instruction *(tôrâ)* of Moses. This is our fourth statement. These instructions are not so much "laws" in the strictly delimited legal sense as they are the way to life with God. They are all to be observed, whether casuistic or apodictic in form, whether ethical or ritual in content, because they come from God as given to Moses. "It is because the covenant relationship is based on personal fidelity that there can be laws whose only 'explanation' is the unfathomable decree of God."[44] This personal fidelity is the basis and lifeblood of Israel's social ethics. Moshe Weinfeld, in his study of social justice, sees the difference between Mesopotamian kings and Israel to lie not in specific actions on behalf of the poor and less fortunate classes as in the foundation, fulfillment of the divine commandment in the covenant, and so in the motivation, service of YHWH rather than self-aggrandizement or preservation of the status quo.[45] Israel's calling is to love loyalty (*ḥesed* as at Mic 6:8) and to know YHWH (Hos 6:3).[46]

This brings us to our fifth and final statement, that the "distinctiveness" of Israel's covenant is *moral* response and commitment. Worship of YHWH (cultic or ritual *tôrâ*) and service of YHWH in the neighbor (ethical or social *tôrâ*) are inseparable. The prophetic critique of cultic practice (e.g., Isa 1:10-17; Jer 7:1-7; Hos 6:6; Amos 5:21-24; Mic 6:6-8; Mal 3:1-5) was aimed precisely at this inseparability. According to Abraham Heschel, the fundamental meaning of justice *(mišpāṭ),* "as an interpersonal relationship," involving claims and responsibilities for both God and the people, "refers to all actions which contribute to maintaining the covenant," i.e., the whole of the community's life in its relation to God and to one another.[47] There is in this an ineluctable concentration on human response and responsibility. As Rabbi Irving Greenberg puts it, the covenantal way reveals the divine commitment to human process. "The central point of the covenant process itself is that despite having all the power to do what God chooses, God has chosen to make the divinely desired outcome dependent on human capacities and efforts."[48]

Ernest Nicholson's whole book moves toward this conclusion. He sees the decisive stage in the emergence of covenantal language to be the eighth-century prophets. However this may be, it is certainly true that the prophets developed and sharpened the meaning of the covenant by their concern with YHWH's justice and the corresponding communal and personal responsibility of the people.

> The conclusion to which this book has led is that covenant-language served as the focal point for that desacralization of a religious society of which the prophets were the chief agents. The concept of a covenant between Yahweh and Israel is, in terms of "cash-value," the concept that religion is based, not on a natural or ontological equivalence between the divine realm and the human, but on *choice:* God's choice of his people and their "choice" of him, that is, their free decision to be obedient and faithful to him. Thus understood, "covenant" is the central expression of the distinctive faith of Israel as "the people of Yahweh," the children of God by adoption and free decision rather than by nature or necessity.[49]

To be effective in this world, Israel's allegiance to YHWH alone, its loyalty, its love and service, must issue in the corporate embodiment of justice. It is to the integration of fidelity and justice in Israel's life with God that we now turn. Israel's true freedom, as is the case with all true freedom, is not simply the freedom to choose. It is the freedom that comes in actually choosing the way of YHWH, the way that is "right" and "just." Any other choice is a return to the slavery of Egypt. YHWH chooses carefully those who by their trials will fulfill his justice; YHWH experiences great anguish when those whom he has chosen fail to remain loyal to him.[50] In the prophetic tradition, the prophet Jeremiah voices the ultimate calamity, that YHWH would break his covenant with Israel (Jer 14:21c), that YHWH would take away his peace, his loyalty and compassion (Jer 16:5c). "Awful as God's punishment would be, to be abandoned by Him would be incomparably worse. The prophet was haunted by the fear of ultimate calamity: God's rejection or loathing of the people."[51] The only thing that can sustain the covenant relationship is the practice of justice.

Justice in the biblical tradition, as J.P.M. Walsh shows, is a matter of power. He describes *mišpāṭ* as "having the say." Though variously translated as judgment, rule, or authority, it should not be taken in a narrow legal sense. It embraces all those ways we construct society, be they political, economic, social, religious. YHWH's *mišpāṭ* is ultimately his governance of the entire created world, though it is given shape in very specific and concrete ways in the life of his people. Correspondingly, Walsh describes *ṣedeq/ṣĕdāqâ* as a "shared sense" ("con-sensus"), a common vision about what is right and good. Again, though variously translated as justice or righteousness, it should not be reduced to a forensic meaning or to an abstract, philosophical concept (commutative or distributive justice). In sum:

> We go along, then, with what we are told to do because it seems right to us. We accept someone's exercise of *mišpāṭ* because it seems to us to accord with *ṣedeq*. We resist *mišpāṭ* when it seems to us to go against *ṣedeq*. And that sense of *ṣedeq* is mediated to us by our participation in our community, as it also defines the consensus that holds a community together.[52]

In addition, the desire to uphold *ṣedeq* is captured in the Hebrew word *nāqām*, which in a positive sense means the vindication of what is right or of the person who is in the right *(ṣaddîq)* and in a negative sense vengeance for what is wrong or upon the person who is in the wrong *(rāšāᶜ)*.

YHWH's *ṣĕdāqâ* is an alternative vision that is communicated through the power of the exodus story. Recall that Genesis 15:6 can be translated: "and Abraham reckoned it to YHWH as *ṣĕdāqâ*." Surely, it is YHWH's vision of Abraham's future and Abraham's willingness to entrust himself to that vision (which only gradually unfolds) that constitutes Abraham's *ṣĕdāqâ*. "Human righteousness for Israel was rooted in God's righteousness, conceived either as gracious saving activity or as a gracious revelation of what is right."[53] In the Exodus experience, YHWH's *ṣĕdāqâ* is first his saving activity (which includes his self-revelation as *ʾehyeh* to Moses) and then his revelation of what is right, his *mišpāṭ* at Sinai. YHWH's *ṣĕdāqâ* could be characterized as his creative and imaginative vision for the whole world. Comprehensively, God established his *mišpāṭ* when he created the world, revealed his *mišpāṭ* at Sinai, and will judge the nations at the eschaton according to his *mišpāṭ wĕṣĕdāqâ*.[54]

How then has YHWH organized this particular society, nation, people, family Israel? Assuming the complex historical development of Israel's identity and sense of justice, including its acceptance of others' views of social justice, its adaptations of these views, and its transformation of them as crises arose,[55] we will focus on two essential factors: Israel as a "divinely willed contrast society" and the need for its own proper form of institutionalization if justice is to be sustainable and efficacious.

Norbert Lohfink advocates the first as we have seen. The experience of the Exodus is the experience of a people set apart, removed from the situation of oppression (historically, both in Canaan and in Egypt), and brought to Sinai in order to worship and serve YHWH alone. This is the period of the tribal league when "there was no king in Israel" (Judg 21:25). Although the book of Judges presents the period as one of struggle to remain loyal to YHWH, it is also, ideally, a period when YHWH alone rules over the people (Judg 8:23) and when YHWH raises up "judges" (2:16: *šōpĕṭîm,* which is the same root, *špṭ,* as *mišpāṭ*) who, inspired by his spirit (3:10), are better termed deliverers or redeemers of the people. When the people want "a king to govern us, like the other nations," it is viewed at least in one strand of the tradition as being a rejection of YHWH "from being king over them" (1 Sam 8:4-22). Israel was supposed to be different, in contrast to the other nations. And Israel survived the tragic history of the monarchy and the collapse of the politico-social and religious structures at the time of the exile because the prophets recalled the primary ethical paradigm. The "royal paradigm visualizes a king who subjects himself to God, upholds justice, and thereby creates shalom. The content of royal justice is provided by Torah, Israel's narrative and legal tradition whose ethic we have earlier characterized as the familial paradigm." The "prophetic paradigm," on the other hand, is a unique calling by God to exhort leaders in other realms (priests, sages, kings) to live as holy, wise, just. Thus, as in the case of Naboth's vineyard (1 Kgs 21:1-29), "God sends a prophetic word when life has been violated, when inheritance/land has been alienated, and when hospitality has been replaced by egotistic concern for self."[56] This deep-rootedness in the story of liberation as a matter of equal rights and duties among the people because all are completely devoted to God's covenantal will is what makes Israel unique among the nations.

But the prophetic word about justice, and this is our second essential factor, is ineffective unless it takes institutional form. This is a matter of structures, legal, social, economic, political, religious, if there is to be sustainable and efficacious justice. True prophets will always be prophets like Moses, whose sole authority comes from the words that YHWH commands (Deut 13:1-5; 18:15-22). These words, even for later prophets, are always the *tôrâ* of Moses as seen in the light of a particular social development or crisis. If not, the prophetic word will have no real and lasting impact. Yairah Amit contrasts the meager influence of prophets who did not attempt "to solve the problem of the gap between the classes through the proposal of a new and different socioeconomic order" with the biblical legal system, which proposes concrete practices (sabbath, sabbatical, jubilee) but encounters difficulty in enforcing the laws (e.g., the debt moratorium at Deut 15:1-11 becomes debt cancellation at Neh 10:32, but then becomes circumvention of the law in Hillel's *prosbol*). Amit sees the jubilee law (Lev 25:10ff.) as an attempt to diminish gaps and to prevent economic inequality, exploitation, and domination (e.g., debts that lead to slavery). Unlike Babylonian and Assyrian edicts which depended on the will or decree of the king and could not be anticipated, jubilee became a "sacred cyclical law" in which the source of power is God, not the king, because the land and the people belong to God. Therefore, it "expresses the desire to create a different society." In sum: "It would appear, therefore, that the jubilee law is a relatively late law, legislated under the influence of the violation of laws which preceded it and in the hope of shaping a different reality."[57]

Another example that both recalls an idealized past of justice and equality and projects a utopian future is the allotment of the land among the tribes (Num 26:52-58; Josh 13:1–21:45; Ezek 47:13–48:29). Shmuel Ahituv concludes his study of the relationship between land and justice:

> While the biblical description of the allotment of the Land of Canaan to the tribes of Israel is not a historical account, it reflects historical situations and cultural and social concepts. Its historical and social background is the tribal-communal organization of the Judahite-Israelite peasantry. Even after the system collapsed with the destruction of the kingdoms of Israel and Judah, its ideas were still fostered. It is possible that it assumed a utopian form when it was no longer implemented in reality. Its principles of justice and equality were projected backwards to the forefathers in the heroic period, to Moses and Joshua, at the very beginning of the national history. Let me suggest that by projecting these ideas back to the venerated past, the authors had in

> mind not only the past, but also, without articulating it, the future, as was done by Ezekiel.[58]

The point is, whether it is a question of jubilee law or land distribution, whether it is a question in either case of an idealized past or a utopian future, such laws in some form must be "implemented in reality" if YHWH's *mišpāṭ* is to be sustained and his *ṣedeq* to be efficacious. In these terms, the people of YHWH have not only a past, but a future.

"A Land Flowing with Milk and Honey": Israel's Destiny

In the wake of the disastrous experience of the exile, Israel will have a future to the degree that it returns to the ideal of covenantal fidelity expressed in the Mosaic covenant but envisioned now as the restoration of creation on God's holy mountain where Abraham bound Isaac and Solomon built the Temple (2 Chr 3:1), and which Ezekiel envisions as the center of the nations (5:5) and the navel *(tabbûr)* of the earth (38:12).[59] As heir to Sinai, Zion must always listen to the voice of Moses, but there has been a shift from Sinai to Zion as the meeting place between heaven and earth. The biblical notion of justice includes not only Israel's relationship to YHWH in covenantal fidelity but also Israel's relationship to other peoples or nations as well as to the whole of creation. How is that relationship to be understood? The fulfillment of Israel's calling to be a light to the nations and Israel's destiny to possess the paradisiacal land flowing with milk and honey revolves around three considerations: (1) the fate of Torah within Israel; (2) the fate of Israel as the Suffering Servant; and (3) the fate of YHWH as the only king in Israel. All three overlap and should be seen in relation to each other, but for the sake of clarity we will consider each in turn by looking at the texts of Isaiah that are pre-exilic, then exilic, and finally post-exilic.

The book of Isaiah is concerned with Israel's relationship to the nations more than any other biblical book. In a famous pre-exilic text, the prophet says:

> In the days to come the mountain of the LORD's house shall be established as the highest of the mountains, and shall be raised above the hills; all the nations shall stream to it. Many peoples shall come and say, "Come, let us go up to the mountain of the LORD, to the house of the God of Jacob; that he may teach us his ways and that we may walk in his paths." For out of Zion shall go forth instruction, and the word of the LORD from Jerusalem. He shall judge between the nations, and shall arbitrate for many peoples; they shall beat their swords into plowshares, and their spears into pruning hooks; nation shall not lift up sword against nation, neither shall they learn war any more (Isa 2:2-4; cp. Mic 4:1-4).

God has a teaching/instruction *(tôrâ)* for the nations which is placed in parallel with God's word (v. 3c). It is related to Israel's *tôrâ* but is not immediately identified with the *tôrâ* of Moses nor connected to the covenant. It is specified as God's judgment (*šāpaṭ* at v. 4), calling the nations to a new way of acting: the cessation of war to bring in the age of peace. But this will depend upon whether "the faithful city" can recover her lost justice *(mišpāṭ)* and righteousness (*ṣedeq:* 1:21; cf. 1:16-17, 23c, 26-27). Isaiah puts it most poignantly in the song of the vineyard (5:1-7), culminating in the devastating word-play (v. 7): "He [YHWH] expected justice *[mišpāṭ]*, but saw bloodshed *[mispāḥ]*; righteousness *[ṣĕdāqâ]*, but heard a cry *[sĕʿāqâ]*!" Lohfink comments on Isaiah 2:2-4 and Micah 4:1-4:

> The logic is: we must now become a just society so that what God will bring about in days to come can thereby begin. That the mountain with the house of YHWH towers above the other hills is dependent on the fate of the torah in Israel. Only when it begins to give light there can the Zion-torah go forth from Israel into the world of the nations.[60]

This is not to deny that the covenant at Sinai was established with Israel alone and that it is Israel's unique prerogative to serve YHWH by observing the *tôrâ* of Moses. It is to say, especially from the analysis of Isaiah and some of the Psalms, that—however unspecified the relationship may be—the nations of the world must be included in YHWH's original intention for the reign of justice and peace. The fundamental theme of the whole book by Norbert Lohfink and Erich Zenger is that "without Israel and its Torah there is no universal salvation from the hand of God."[61]

Moving to the time of the exile, according to Second Isaiah (Isaiah 40–55), it is YHWH's servant Israel who will teach justice *(mišpāṭ)* to the nations (42:1, 3, 4). They await his *tôrâ* (v. 4; cf. 51:4). Yet this servant is poor and suffering. Is this a new identity for Israel or part of its original destiny? Lohfink in his Bailey Lectures on the option for the poor in the Bible sees in the prophet Zephaniah a pre-exilic affirmation of the new Jerusalem as "a city of the poor of Yahweh." This is based on the reversal of the day of YHWH culminating in 3:12-13. "For I will leave in the midst of you a people humble *[ʿānî]* and lowly [or poor: *dāl*]. They shall seek refuge in the name of the LORD—the remnant of Israel." Lohfink notes that this is "the first time the theme of God's concern for the poor appears as the coming hope of Israel." The immediate focus is on the poor and exploited within Israel, but the horizon in Zephaniah embraces all the societies of the earth (3:8-10).[62]

This initial indication in Zephaniah becomes thematic in Second Isaiah. At the Exodus YHWH rescued his people from poverty and oppression to become a contrast-society in which there are no poor, but their failure to embrace and live this *mišpāṭ* of YHWH has resulted in YHWH's wrath so that in the exile YHWH has made Israel poor and oppressed (Isa 40:2; 42:18-25; 43:22-28; 47:6-9; 48:1-22; 50:1-3; 51:17-23). But the nations, especially Babylon (47:1-15), have gone too far and treated Israel unjustly so that YHWH will take vengeance (*nāqām* at 47:3) in order to restore Israel (48:1-22) characterized by its lack of fidelity *(ʾĕmet)* and righteousness (*ṣĕdāqâ* at 48:1: cf. 54:14, 17). As at the Exodus, YHWH alone, creator and redeemer, can do this, but he does it by making Israel his own nation in, as Lohfink says, "a second and unique sense." All Israel is now the poor, suffering people of YHWH, YHWH's servant who will teach justice to the nations (42:1-4) and will not only "raise up the tribes of Jacob" and "restore the survivors of Israel," but will be "a light to the nations" so that YHWH's salvation "may reach to the ends of the earth" (49:6).[63] Hence, Israel as the suffering servant reveals to the nations their own violence and injustice (50:4-11; 52:13-15). He does so as well to those within Israel who cannot accept their identity with the suffering poor and/or cannot see such suffering as redemptive (53:1-9). But it is God's will that through his suffering/knowledge "the righteous one *[ṣaddîq]*, my servant, will make many righteous" (53:11). Lohfink concludes:

> Yahweh's plan is now more comprehensive than in the first Exodus. If at that time he planned to constitute, at last, a just people in contrast to the other nations, this time he makes the nation created out of his poor to be a model for all societies. . . . In the end, the reconstitution of the Yahweh-society out of poor and persecuted Israel promotes the transformation of the whole of world society.

But, he asks, has this good news been fulfilled or does it await a more distant future?[64]

Moving as our third consideration to the post-exilic period, represented here by Third Isaiah (Isaiah 56–66), there is an increasing emphasis on YHWH as the only one who rules in Israel. As a collection of miscellaneous post-exilic oracles (according to the NRSV), Third Isaiah continues many of the themes of Second Isaiah, especially the central and vital significance of *mišpāṭ wĕṣĕdāqâ* (56:1; 58:2, 6-12; 59:8-19), but in place of the suffering servant it is now YHWH alone who will redeem Zion (59:16-17, 20). All peoples are included if they hold fast to YHWH's covenant (56:1-7), but the central image is the new and glorious Jerusalem that YHWH will create (60:1-22; v. 19c: "the LORD will be your everlasting light, and your God will be your glory"). Isaiah 61:1-7 is the closest Third Isaiah comes to the servant songs of Second Isaiah, but the one anointed by the spirit of YHWH is sent to proclaim the good news of YHWH's salvific activity for Zion: "to proclaim the year of the

LORD's favor, and the day of vengeance [or, vindication: *nāqām*] of our God. . . . For I the LORD love justice *[mišpāṭ]*" (vv. 2, 8). That vindication of divine justice recalls God's mighty saving acts with Moses in the Exodus (63:7-14) as the basis for future hope (63:15–64:12). The promise is for those who consent *(ṣaddîqîm)* to YHWH's vision of things *(mišpāṭ)*. "I will bring forth descendants from Jacob, and from Judah inheritors of my mountains; my chosen shall inherit it, and my servants shall settle there" (65:9). YHWH will create "new heavens and a new earth" (65:17), which is described as the paradisiacal land of joy and peace, Jerusalem, God's "holy mountain" (65:25). YHWH's voice is heard again in the Temple (66:6) and all nations, "all flesh," shall come to worship (66:23). Ezekiel too concludes his vision of the restored Temple and land with the simple words: "And the name of the city from that time on shall be, The LORD is There" (Ezek 48:35).[65]

The land belongs to YHWH. The destiny of Israel is to live where YHWH dwells (Isa 1:26-27; 60:14; 62:1-12; Jer 3:17; 23:6; Ezek 48:35; Zech 8:1-8). This is Zion, the city of YHWH, where YHWH's faithful love *(ḥesed wĕ ʾĕmet)* establishes the eternal covenant of justice and peace. The witness of the prophets and the psalms are in the end commentary on the five books of Moses (the Pentateuch or Torah). In a collection of interesting essays on the priestly narrative (P^g) and on the book of Deuteronomy, Norbert Lohfink opens up a view of P^g that allows us to see differing views within the Pentateuch on the structures (monarchy and Temple), and so on the destiny, of Israel. The differences come into clearest focus in his chapter on "The Strata of the Pentateuch and the Question of War."[66] He sees the deuteronomic narrative of the occupation of the land (Deut 1:1–Josh 22:34 designated as "DtrL"), with its "perfectly ruthless theology of war," as having a very precise political application: to justify Josiah's policies of rebuilding the structure of plausibility within Judah through the law and of extending that law outward, especially to the north, through territorial expansion.

The priestly historical narrative eliminates war from the story it tells (cf. Isa 2:2-4), beginning with the creation of the world and moving through the history of human sin and of the people of Israel. YHWH alone combats chaos (e.g., the sea) and YHWH alone judges and punishes sin. For P^g there are three "original sins" based on its thoroughgoing "history of origins": (1) the sin of violence against fellow human beings (Gen 6:11-13) that corrupts God's good creation (especially by destroying *life*); (2) the sin of slander against the land that denies God's good gift on the part of the representative leadership of the people (Num 13:32; 14:36-37); and (3) the sin of failure to *trust* in YHWH's power and to *honor* YHWH as the Holy One before the people on the part of Moses and Aaron (Num 20:12).[67] The latter might be seen as a failure to honor the kinship relationship of the covenant. Life, land (including hospitality), and kinship mark Israel's unique relationship with YHWH. For the post-exilic author of P^g, the societal structure of peace and stability centers around harmony, based on the heavenly model of God's original creation, through worship and the power of ritual. The purpose or end of human history is the meeting of heaven and earth in an earthly sanctuary (the Temple) modeled on the heavenly sanctuary (Exodus 25–31; 36–40).[68] There is a move in Israel's structures from tribal society to monarchy to Temple. All are included in the final canonical form of the Pentateuch, but the vision that the priestly author offers is distinctive:

> In the wake of the egalitarian, but externally fortified and even aggressive tribal agrarian society, there had been an attempt to create a just state whose king would rule, according to the pattern of other kings, in the name of YHWH. The final ideological elaboration of this society was the deuteronomic project. After the collapse of the state, what emerged was a strongly sacralized sub-society, living around the Jerusalem temple as a kind of enclave within the larger framework of an imperial world society.[69]

And so it was in Jesus' day. As we turn to Jesus' proclamation of the good news of YHWH's salvific activity (Isa 61:1-7; Luke 4:16-21), we wish to investigate whether and how that proclamation corresponds to the idea of justice in the Hebrew Bible. By way of conclusion to this chapter, let us consider the key points that may find correspondence in the aims and concerns of Jesus. First, the blessing of Jacob-Israel is that YHWH alone is king in Israel, not therefore the imperial power or the Temple aristocracy. In place of the elite, this implies a return in some sense to the *ideals* of the tribal league.

Second, YHWH calls Israel forth from oppression and slavery to be a people set apart, a contrast-society, among whom there should be no more poverty and oppression. But, through the experience of exile, Israel itself becomes poor and oppressed, the suffering servant, whom YHWH chooses in a new way to reveal to the nations their own violence and injustice. From the Exodus to the exile, YHWH's initiatives of grace call for a human response of turning and trusting in absolute obedience. This is a communal/corporate embodiment ("con-sensus") of covenantal loyalty that alone can sustain justice.

Third, the question of who belongs to YHWH's reign/kingdom is not finally dependent on particular structures such as the monarchy or the priesthood, but it must take some institutional or societal form. To be effective YHWH's and Israel's *ṣĕdāqâ* must take the concrete and specific shape of YHWH's *mišpāṭ*. Israel survived the desolating experience of exile, the loss of monarchy and Temple, because it had the *tôrâ* of Moses.

This is what constitutes Israel's unique and distinctive identity as the family of YHWH (kinship, life, land, and hospitality).

Fourth, the concrete and specific hope for the return to Zion was never lost from sight as the psalms and the prophets demonstrate, but it is YHWH's return, and only that, that can reconstitute Israel. This can only be a return to YHWH's original intention at the creation and the Exodus. It is a return to the covenant of the heart (Jer 31:31-34), to the deeper sense of harmony and non-violence (Isa 2:2-4) that will usher in the universal reign of justice, peace, and joy. The question that Malachi puts on the lips of the people, "Where is the God of justice?" is the same question in Jesus' day. How he answered that question is the subject of the next chapter. As a transitional appendix, we will offer a reading of the book of Malachi which constitutes a prophetic commentary on the *tôrâ* (teaching/instruction) of Moses amid the continuing ambiguity of the post-exilic period.

Appendix: Malachi: The Last of the Writing Prophets

In the Christian canon, the book of Malachi is the final book that prepares the way for John the Baptist and Jesus. In the Tanakh, the Hebrew canon, it is the last book of the prophets. Canonically, the prophetic books *(Neviʾim)* are framed by references to "Moses the servant of the LORD" (Josh 1:1) and "the teaching *[tôrâ]* of my servant Moses" (Mal 4:4 [3:22 MT]). Likewise, the last word of Moses in the Torah is a blessing: "Happy are you, O Israel" (Deut 33:29), and the first word of the Writings *(Kethuvim)* is also a blessing: "Happy are those . . ." (Ps 1:1). Psalm 1 follows Malachi as a thematic restatement of the distinction between the wicked whose way is doomed by judgment *(bamišpāṭ)* and the righteous *(ṣaddîqîm)* whose delight is in the *tôrâ* of YHWH. For Malachi the *tôrâ* is inseparable from fidelity to the covenant.[70]

The word *malʾākî* means "my messenger" (or "angel") and occurs at 1:1; 3:1 (twice), while at 2:7 a priest is called "the messenger of the LORD of Hosts." Some identify the messenger of 3:1 with Elijah at 4:5 (3:23 MT) because the same sending formula is used in both texts ("Behold, I am sending . . ."). Nothing is known of the author, but the text reflects the period of reform after the rebuilding of the Temple was started, either before or after the time of Ezra and Nehemiah (ca. 450 B.C.E.?). The voice we hear is both priestly and prophetic. As such it "encourages continued dialogue" between both.[71] The NRSV sees one central theme as dominating: fidelity to the Lord's covenant and its teachings *(tôrâ)*. Yet the mood is one of disillusionment and demoralization in the face of abuses, particularly in the Temple administration and in the taking of foreign wives. The text is thus a call to reform in the face of perceived infidelity, but more to the point as a transition to the next chapter on Jesus, the theological themes that the author brings into play form a sort of reprise and evocation of the history of Israel from the blessing of Jacob to the arrival of the God of justice, the day of the Lord of Hosts.

Structurally, Malachi divides into six oracles followed by two appendices. The author employs a question-answer format. All the oracles except the third begin with a statement from YHWH, and all include an implicitly self-condemnatory question from the people (Israel at 1:1) in the formula: "But you say . . . ." What follows is a brief summary of the main themes.

Oracle 1 (1:2-5): YHWH has loved Jacob and hated Esau (cf. Rom 9:13), which addresses both the election of Israel and the condemnation of nations (Edom) who have opposed Israel. YHWH's great power reaches beyond the borders of Israel (v. 5).

Oracle 2 (1:6–2:9): YHWH is father and master whose name is reverenced among the nations (1:11, 14), but despised among the priests who do not fulfill the cultic requirements of the Mosaic law. This evokes the exodus experience as does the command to continue the covenant with Levi, a covenant of life *(ḥayyîm)* and of well being *(šālôm)* and of true reverence for the name, a covenant of true instruction *(tôrâ)* and complete loyalty. "For the lips of a priest should guard knowledge, and people should seek instruction *[tôrâ]* from his mouth, for he is the messenger of the LORD of hosts" (2:7). The covenant with Levi recalls the priestly genealogy (Exod 6:14-27) that indicates both Moses and Aaron belong to the tribe of Levi. Moreover, it evokes the tribe's zeal and loyalty to YHWH, which brought it a blessing (Exod 32:25-29; Deut 33:8-11). There are strong echoes in this text of Jeremiah 33:14-26 (v. 18: "levitical priests"; v. 21: "my covenant with my ministers the Levites"; v. 22: "the offspring of the Levites"; v. 26: "the offspring of Jacob"). Both Jeremiah and Malachi may represent a dissident critique of the Zadokite priesthood. In any event, moving from Jacob in the first oracle to Levi in the second recalls the twelve tribes of the Exodus experience and their worship (service) of YHWH in both cult and instruction *(tôrâ)* as mediated through the sons of Levi, Moses, and Aaron, an ideal time to which Israel must return if the name of YHWH is to be reverenced in Israel as it is, to their shame, among the nations.

Oracle 3 (2:10-16): YHWH is the one father, the one God who has created Israel, so Israel is called to be faithful in their relations to one another and to honor the "covenant of our fathers" *(bĕrît ʾăbōtênû)*. The occasion is marriage with foreign wives, but the emphasis is on covenantal fidelity (v. 14: "your wife by covenant"), which reaches back to the original divine intention at the beginning of creation (the threefold play on *rûaḥ* [life-breath] at vv. 15-16 recalls Gen 1:2; 2:7). Also, the rabbinic tradition sees the call of Abraham and the covenant with him and his descendants as the beginning of the restoration of creation after the history of human sinfulness (Gen 1-11; 12:1ff.). Crucially significant for our later discussion is that YHWH and Israel form one family. They have a kinship relationship.

Oracle 4 (2:17–3:5): YHWH is wearied by their cynical words: "All who do evil are good in the sight of the LORD, and he delights in them," and their cynical question: "Where is the God of justice?" So YHWH is sending his messenger to prepare the way, the messenger of the covenant whom they desire but will not be able to endure, for he will purify "the descendants of Levi" until they present offerings to YHWH in "righteousness" (v. 3: *biṣĕdāqâ*), which will be pleasing to YHWH as in the days of old. All of this culminates in verse 5 when YHWH "will suddenly come to his temple" (3:1): "Then I will draw near to you for judgment *[lamišpāṭ]*. I will be swift to bear witness against the sorcerers, against the adulterers, against those who swear falsely, against those who oppress the hired workers in their wages, the widow and the orphan, against those who thrust aside the alien, and do not fear me, says the LORD of hosts." Here in brief compass we have the traditional prophetic concern for YHWH's *mišpāṭ*. Sorcerers would be those who make use of idols or magic. Adulterers are those who are not faithful in their marital relationships as addressed in the third oracle. Those who swear falsely are those who practice various forms of injustice in the courts. The hired workers, widows, orphans, and aliens are the most vulnerable in society and most in need of protection from oppressors. Those who do not fear or reverence YHWH refers particularly to the priests mentioned in the second oracle. Thus, the answer to their cynical statement and question is the swift and sure execution of YHWH's *mišpāṭ*.

Oracle 5 (3:6-12): YHWH does not change, so the children of Jacob have not perished even though from the days of their fathers they have turned away from YHWH's statutes *(ḥuqqây)*. Hence, the possibility of turning *(šûb)* is offered: "Return to me and I will return to you, says the LORD of hosts" (v. 7). The immediate exhortation is to observe the cultic statutes for tithes and offerings and so receive the promise of "an overflowing blessing" (v. 10), which, by implication, is the paradisiacal land flowing with milk and honey. "Then all nations will count you happy, for you will be a land of delight, says the LORD of hosts" (v. 12). Eden (Gen 2:8-9) means delight. This is Israel's destiny: to live where YHWH dwells, in the land that belongs to YHWH alone (Isa 62:2-5, 12).

Oracle 6 (3:13–4:3 [3:13-21 MT]): YHWH's day of judgment will come, nonetheless, and it will reveal "the difference between the righteous and the wicked, between one who serves God and one who does not serve him" (3:18). Striking here is the distinction within Israel itself of those who fear or reverence YHWH and those who remain in their wickedness. YHWH says of "those who revered the LORD and thought on his name" (v. 16): "They shall be mine, says the LORD of hosts, my special possession *[sĕgūllâ]* on the day when I act, and I will spare them as parents spare their children who serve them" (v. 17). YHWH's special care and election of Israel (Exod 19:5; Deut 7:6; 14:2; 26:18; Ps 135:4) is now focused on those who reverence his name and serve him faithfully. They are to him as his own children and he is their parent. YHWH's special kinship with Israel continues in the healing and vindication symbolized by "the sun of righteousness" (*šemeš ṣĕdāqâ* at 4:2 [3:20 MT]).

Appendix 1 (4:4 [3:22 MT]): In all of this, if there is one thing the people are to remember it is "the teaching *[tôrâ]* of my servant Moses, the statutes *[ḥuqqîm]* and ordinances *[mišpāṭîm]* that I commanded him at Horeb for all Israel." This is the first explicit mention of Moses, but it is clear that the Mosaic law with its originating covenant is the leitmotif of the entire book. Moses continues to be the leader of all Israel in the Second Temple period, as is evident not only from the text of Malachi but from the canonical connections in the Tanakh as outlined above.

Appendix 2 (4:5-6 [3:23-24 MT]): This final word may seem like an appendix, yet it says the one thing that must be said. Elijah the prophet represents the continuing prophetic critique of those who do not fulfill YHWH's *mišpāṭ* and so are not prepared for "the great and terrible day of the LORD." What is the one thing necessary? That Israel be and remain YHWH's own kin and so a family in which parents and children love one another. This requires a turning *(šûb)* of the heart which the prophet will effect to avoid the opposite, the utter destruction *(ḥerem)* of the land. The word *ḥerem* is the last word written by Malachi. It conjures up a devastating image of the possible reversal of the promise of divine blessing. The Christian Scriptures in the Lukan tradition see a positive fulfillment of Elijah's role in John the Baptist: "He will turn many of the people of Israel to the Lord their God. With the spirit and power of Elijah he will go before him, to turn the hearts of parents to their children, and the disobedient to the wisdom of the righteous, to make ready a people prepared for the Lord" (Luke 1:16-17).

Malachi is an intriguing and challenging book. As a testimony of the last of the prophets, it brings together the major themes of Israel's self-understanding: election as children of Jacob; the Exodus experience and its demand for fidelity to the covenant as expressed in Mosaic law and cult, particularly reverence for the Name; the foundational image of YHWH and Israel as kin, as family in which love and service of YHWH is expressed in love and service of one another; the ineluctable significance of righteousness *(ṣĕdāqâ)* and justice *(mišpāṭ)* if such love and service is to be effective; the possibility of conversion *(šûb)* to realize the promises and blessings of YHWH; the inescapable day of YHWH that will separate righteous and wicked even within Israel itself; through it all, YHWH's continued election of the righteous *(ṣaddîqîm)* as his special possession *(sĕgūllâ)*. Those who would be such must do two things: remember the *tôrâ* of Moses and experience a turning of the heart. This last can be understood as faithful love *(ḥesed wĕʾĕmet)*, which is not mentioned as such in this text but is at the heart of Israel's self-understanding.

Is the perspective of Malachi, and indeed of the Hebrew canon, particularist or universalist? Actually, the alternatives are not viable insofar as true universality demands and always occurs in intense particularity.[72] Malachi reflects what is deepest and best in the traditions and history of Israel. It is only by entering more deeply into Israel's relationship to YHWH, particularly in terms of covenantal fidelity, that we can understand the notion of justice at the center of that relationship and how that notion of justice extends outward and affects Israel's relationship to other people and/or nations. The questions to YHWH that he puts on the lips of the people should continue to haunt both Jews and Christians: "How have you loved us?" (1:2); "How have we despised your name?" (1:6); "Why does he not (accept the offerings with favor)?" (2:14); "Where is the God of justice?" (2:17); "How shall we return?" (3:7); "How have we spoken against you?" (3:13). Israel has a unique relationship to YHWH, but the questions posed resonate in all human hearts. As Abraham Heschel has said so well: "The situation of a person immersed in the prophets' words is one of being exposed to a ceaseless shattering of indifference, and one needs a skull of stone to remain callous to such blows." The blows come from the fact that the prophet "discloses *a divine pathos*, not just a divine judgment," that "the fundamental experience of the prophet is a fellowship with the feelings of God . . . ."[73] In focusing on the Torah (Pentateuch), we must keep ever in mind the prophetic concern to remind the people of YHWH's personal and passionate involvement in their lives and their history. This, we propose, is what Jesus was sent to do.

Notes

[1] Michael A. Signer, "One Covenant or Two: Can We Sing a New Song?" *Reinterpreting Revelation and Tradition: Jews and Christians in Conversation*, ed. John T. Pawlikowski and Hayim Goren Perelmuter (Franklin, Wisc.: Sheed & Ward, 2000) 8. Signer proposes a dynamic movement of "turning" *(teshuvah)* as Israel faces its creator, turns to other peoples, and recognizes its scriptures in

others. The third turning is a "turning together to be a blessing" both to one another (Jews and Christians) and then to all the nations "grounded in the reality of a reciprocal relationship between Jews and Christians" based in "their common root," i.e., "their traditions of interpreting the Hebrew Bible" (18).

[2] John T. Pawlikowski, "The Search for a New Paradigm for the Christian-Jewish Relationship: A Response to Michael Signer," ibid., 25–48, offers a very helpful review of various authors who hold "the single covenant model" and those who hold a "double covenant perspective." He concludes: "The double covenantal model, despite its evident drawbacks, more faithfully represents the reality of the Christian-Jewish relationship both historically and theologically. Too many of single covenant proponents are excessively locked into a biblical framework" (40). He may well be right from the perspective of the whole history of Jewish-Christian relations, but our concern is with Jesus before the advent of Christianity, a time when there was only one covenant to which all other expressions related: the Mosaic covenant.

[3] The NRSV notes that the meaning of the phrase "a covenant to the people" is uncertain in Hebrew. The NJPS translates it as "a covenant people" but notes that literally it means "covenants of a people," although the meaning of the Hebrew is uncertain. The Hebrew for both phrases is *libĕrît ʿām lĕʾôr gôyīm*. Cf. Isa 49:6, 8. Isa 51:4 says: "Listen to me, my people, and give heed to me, my nation; for a teaching *[tôrâ]* will go out from me, and my justice *[mišpāṭî]* for a light to the peoples *[lĕʾôr ʾammîm]*."

[4] Signer, "One Covenant or Two," comments: "The narrative framework for understanding the relationship of fidelity to the God of Israel among the nations emerges during the interaction between the community in Judea and its neighbors in Syria and Egypt during the Hellenistic period" (9). His concern here is to focus upon the development of Christian and rabbinic views. Our concern is to push the question of Israel's relation to the nations back to the very origins of Israel.

[5] There have been innumerable books published by Jewish and Christian scholars together. Recent examples include *Reinterpreting Revelation and Tradition*, ed. Pawlikowski and Perelmuter, cited above (n. 1), and *Christianity in Jewish Terms*, ed. Tikva Frymer-Kensky, David Novak, Peter Ochs, David Fox Sandmel, Michael A. Signer (Boulder, Colo.: Westview Press, 2000), a book that develops the *Dabru Emet* statement written with the intent of treating Christianity from a Jewish perspective. Norbert Lohfink and Erich Zenger, in *The God of Israel and the Nations: Studies in Isaiah and the Psalms*, trans. Everett R. Kalin (Collegeville: The Liturgical Press, 2000), begin with a chapter entitled "The Theological Context: The New Relationship Between the Church and Israel" (1–7) and, after citing Rolf Rendtorff on "maintaining Israel's identity undiminished," affirm: "It dare no longer be a matter of what sometimes appears as a 'Christian theology of Judaism' that wishes to 'evaluate' Judaism with categories that are 'allegedly' Christian and alien to what is Jewish. In the final analysis, these categories cannot be used because they correspond neither to historical nor theological reality. Rather, what is required is a reflection and, if possible, also a conceptual world that goes back to the common root in which, on the one hand, Jews find themselves again as Jews, *and* in which, on the other hand, the Church holds on to

what distinguishes it from Judaism (its so-called *proprium Christianum*) as well as what binds it to Judaism" (5, emphasis in original). Appealing to the Tanakh (Hebrew canon) as a biblical tradition common to Christians and Jews that can provide biblical "models" usable to both, the book develops a biblical theology of covenant and of Israel's, or the God of Israel's, relation to the nations.

[6] Martin Buber, *Moses: The Revelation and the Covenant* (New York: Harper & Row, 1958; originally published in 1946) 60, outlines the essential elements of the experience as (1) flight into the desert (Exod 1:11-15a); (2) a return to the experience of his ancestors as a shepherd in the land of Midian (Exod 1:15b-22); (3) the central revelatory encounter (Exod 2:23–4:17); (4) an encounter with the demonic (Exod 4:24-26). It is this foundational experience that gives shape and direction to the rest of the narrative. I would add that every great religious figure, whether Moses or Gotama or Jesus or Muhammad, is not so much concerned with "founding a religion" as with communicating a foundational experience that gives shape and direction to everything that emerges later.

[7] See the citation from Jon Levenson in Chapter 1, n. 46 of this book.

[8] Commenting on Ps 62:12 ("God has spoken once, we have heard it twice"), he says: "I would argue that it suggests only one covenant from the perspective of God. This one covenant stands both revealed and concealed in the language of Hebrew Scripture. There are, however, two distinct yet recognizably analogous realizations of the covenant: one in Oral Torah for Jews and one in the incarnate word for Christians." Signer, "One Covenant or Two," 19.

[9] As examples, all from Christian exegetes: Paul D. Hanson, *The People Called: The Growth of Community in the Bible* (San Francisco: Harper & Row, 1986), offers a predominantly diachronic review of the development of community: "An historical development understood in relational-covenantal terms. For example, the universal scope of the biblical notion of community emerged through stages from a narrow clan henotheism through a national cult to a prophetically based and eschatologically oriented universalism" (538). Lohfink and Zenger, in *The God of Israel,* employ a synchronic approach: "In regard to methodology we utilize the concerns of canonical criticism and the more recent reader-response theory because they are especially suitable for a theological reading of the biblical texts" (vii). Norbert Lohfink, *Theology of the Pentateuch: Themes of the Priestly Narrative and Deuteronomy,* trans. Linda M. Maloney (Minneapolis: Fortress Press, 1994) offers focused articles in the style of Albrecht Alt and says of his studies on Deuteronomy: "They are not 'synchronic' in the sense that they only work with the canonical text in its final form, but they do attempt a synchronic view of broader connections and structures in the different diachronic layers of the text" (ix). Waldemar Janzen, *Old Testament Ethics: A Paradigmatic Approach* (Louisville: Westminster/John Knox Press, 1994) 1–6, offers (as the title indicates) a paradigmatic approach: "It is my goal to provide Christians with a model for grasping the Old Testament's ethical message in a comprehensive way, thereby avoiding a reductionist concentration on any one genre, like law, or any one selection of texts, like the Ten Commandments or the prophetic calls for justice." He starts with stories that model "the God-pleasing life" and sees the "familial paradigm" as offering the most comprehensive paradigm. The other paradigms (priestly, wisdom, royal, and prophetic) as subordinate "work together to

uphold" the familial paradigm. Yet his method also includes "a certain dialectical relationship between the completed canon and the history of Israel that led to it" (n. 1). J. David Pleins, *The Social Visions of the Hebrew Bible: A Theological Introduction* (Louisville: Westminster/John Knox Press, 2001), emphasizes the diversity of the Hebrew Bible as "struggle-ridden texts" (28) that calls for employing all the methods of contemporary biblical criticism: "An integrated, sociologically informed, theological-materialist reading of the biblical text, vigorously pursued, will serve as the productive ground for bringing the Hebrew Bible into current theological debates over social ethics" (21). All of these authors emphasize the relevance of their work for contemporary social concerns, employing in one way or another the classical hermeneutical circle of bringing questions to the text and finding that the text has questions for us.

[10] I treat this more fully in *Christology as Narrative Quest* (Collegeville: The Liturgical Press, 1997) 31ff., 70–2, using the insights of Paul Ricoeur and Sandra Schneiders. For a "postcritical" approach that sees both text and intratextual context as having a pragmatic reference, i.e., as performative insofar as the text has practical effects in the conduct and behavior of the community of interpreters, see Peter Ochs, ed., *The Return to Scripture in Judaism and Christianity: Essays in Postcritical Scriptural Interpretation* (Mahwah, N.J.: Paulist Press, 1993).

[11] Pleins, *Social Visions*, 24–8, gives a succinct review of the current state of the question and affirms the continuing validity of the distinctions: "Yet regardless of whether or not we call J, E, D, and P 'sources,' 'tradents,' or 'traditions' (and I intermingle all these designations in this study), the fact of the matter is that in large measure we can discern in these labels competing theological voices that have contributed uniquely to the ongoing discussion of ethical praxis in ancient Israel" (26). He opts for late dating of the materials (largely post-exilic) because he sees the needs and anxieties of the post-exilic age to be dominant, though he does recognize poetic texts such as Exodus 15, Deuteronomy 33, and Judges 5 as attesting "an ancient epic tradition" (27). Frank Moore Cross, *From Epic to Canon: History and Literature in Ancient Israel* (Baltimore: Johns Hopkins University Press, 1998), continues on the other side to affirm the early epic traditions as a source for historical reconstruction: "This volume of essays was designed originally to fill interstices in my earlier study *Canaanite Myth and Hebrew Epic* (Cambridge: Harvard University Press, 1973 [ninth printing, 1997]). The first three essays in particular reflect similar concerns with epic tradition and historical reconstruction" (xi).

In the second essay, "Traditional Narrative and the Reconstruction of Early Israelite Institutions," he affirms: "The epic cycle of old Israel in its mature form was a creation of the Israelite league. It cannot be later than the epic sources of the early monarchy, notably the Yahwistic work from Solomonic times" (43). The question of what we can know about the origins of Israel will be important to our discussion. On the complexities of source criticism, especially "D" and "Dtr," see the collection of essays edited by Linda S. Schearing and Steven L. McKenzie, *Those Elusive Deuteronomists: The Phenomenon of Pan-Deuteronomism* (Sheffield: Sheffield Academic Press, 1999). Although the scholars have differing views and there is no consensus, the general trend of the book is toward recognizing that there is no "Dtr movement" and no "pan-Deuteronomism," but there is clear literary activity and influence on certain texts. Robert A. Kugler, "The Deuteronomists and the Latter Prophets," 127–44, proposes stringent criteria that leave only Amos and Jeremiah as showing Deuteronomic influence. He also suggests that Hosea and Micah may have influenced the Deuteronomic history rather than the other way around. John Van Seters, "Is There Evidence of a Dtr Redaction in the Sinai Pericope (Exodus 19–24, 32–34)?" 160–70, sees "J" as later than "D" and so as taking over and transforming material from "D" or "Dtr."

[12] Lohfink, *Theology of the Pentateuch,* ch. 7: "The Strata of the Pentateuch and the Question of War" (173–226). The citations are on 176 and 201.

[13] Cross, *From Epic to Canon,* ch. 10: "The Fixation of the Text of the Hebrew Bible" (205–18), sees three forms of the text (of the Pentateuch and Samuel) that developed between the fifth and the first centuries B.C.E.: (1) Palestinian found in Chronicles, Qumran, and the Samaritan Pentateuch; (2) Egyptian found in the LXX (Greek translation) with close affinities to the Palestinian; (3) Babylonian found as the base of the rabbinic recension of the Pentateuch and Samuel (212). He goes on to discuss other discoveries (such as the texts found at Wâdi Murabbaʾat in 1961) that indicate a text of "massive authority, at least in the Pharisaic circles, and which came to dominate the Jewish community" between 70 C.E. and 135 C.E. (213). He concludes that the rabbis did not expand or conflate texts, but chose a single textual tradition. This may have begun in the early first century C.E. with Hillel and his disciples who, like Ezra, came to Jerusalem from Babylon. This is "the Pharisaic-Hillelite Recension, of which the Masoretic Text is a direct descendant" (217). Many scholars today see greater fluidity in the process of textual transmission. See, for example, Al Wolters, "The Text of the Old Testament," *The Face of Old Testament Studies: A Survey of Contemporary Approaches,* ed. D. W. Baker and B. T. Arnold (Grand Rapids, Mich.: Baker Books, 1999) 19–37.

[14] Jon D. Levenson, *The Hebrew Bible, the Old Testament, and Historical Criticism* (Louisville: Westminster John Knox Press, 1993) 140ff., outlines three meanings of exodus as (1) *enthronement* of YHWH and glad acceptance of his endless reign by his redeemed people, Israel (cf. Exod 15:17-18 and Psalms 93; 95–99: "YHWH is king"); (2) *covenant* that gives authority to the commandments and ensures their observance with love and gratitude (cf. Exod 19:4-6; Deut 6:20-25); (3) *dedication* in the sense of consecration to the service of YHWH (cf. Lev 25:55; Exod 7:16; 8:1, 8, 20; 9:1, 13; 10:3). Levenson translates the root *ʿbd* in the Exodus texts as "serve" ("Let my people go that they may serve me"), the NRSV as "worship" or "offer sacrifice." Whether translated as service, slavery, or worship, the basic contrast is between serving pharaoh and serving YHWH. Levenson comments: "In their various ways, enthronement, covenant, and dedication all signify God's proprietorship of Israel and Israel's inescapable subjugation to its God" (144).

[15] For a clear and readable review of the various positions taken see John J. McDermott, *What Are They Saying About the Formation of Israel?* (Mahwah, N.J.: Paulist Press, 1998). He discusses three classic models: (1) "conquest" associated with W. F. Albright; (2) "peaceful infiltration" associated with Albrecht Alt and Martin Noth; (3) "social revolution" associated with George Mendenhall and Norman Gottwald. These models have gone through subsequent scholarly

qualifications and, although there is no consensus, many are moving toward the view that "the first Israelites were Canaanites." For a lively discussion among current scholars with diverse views see Hershel Shanks, William G. Dever, Baruch Halpern, P. Kyle McCarter Jr., *The Rise of Ancient Israel* (Washington, D.C.: Biblical Archaeology Society, 1992). For a good summary of current views on *ʿapīru* see Robert B. Coote, "Hapiru, Apiru," *Eerdmans Dictionary of the Bible,* ed. David Noel Freedman (Grand Rapids, Mich.: Eerdmans Publishing, 2000) 549–51.

[16] J.P.M. Walsh, *The Mighty from Their Thrones: Power in the Biblical Tradition* (Philadelphia: Fortress Press, 1987) 47, where he summarizes his view of the relation of "Elohistic Israel" to "Yahwistic Israel." He offers a viable reconstruction centered around his understanding of *ṣedeq* and *mišpāṭ* to which we shall return below. He admits that the reconstruction is based on "guesswork" (38) with many unresolved issues. I have outlined the three historical factors that seem irreducibly necessary to account for both the biblical narrative and the archaeological and historical evidence. There are some who maintain that the Exodus never happened in any sense, but such a view has to ignore the biblical evidence.

[17] P. Kyle McCarter Jr., "The Origins of Israelite Religion," *The Rise of Ancient Israel,* ed. Shanks et al., 131–2.

[18] Trans. of Exod 3:14 my own. The NJPS simply uses "Ehyeh." This text on the call of Moses (Exod 2:23–4:17) is usually attributed to the Elohist (E) and of course was written down long after the connection was made between *ʾel (ʾelohim)* and YHWH. However one understands the experience in the highlands of Canaan, it need not deny an earlier connection. Buber, *Moses,* 49–51, in attempting to explain the discrepancy between Gen 15:7 where Abraham is given the revelation "I am YHWH" and the priestly (P) view of Exod 6:3 that God did not reveal the name YHWH to Abraham, Isaac, and Jacob, appeals to the possibility that the original designation (which would have been similar in Arabic) was something like "Ya-hu," i.e., "O He!" as a cry to the unnamable divinity. As such, it could have been a family tradition that helped prepare the way for, but was not identical to, the revelation given to Moses. The *ʾehyeh* of exodus is the God who will be faithfully present to his people in the midst of their suffering (cf. Hos 1:9 which says: "You are not my people and I will not be *[loʾ-ʾehyeh]* for you"; trans. my own). For Buber, the only possible origin of the name YHWH, however transmitted later, is the religious experience of Moses.

[19] Jon D. Levenson, *The Death and Resurrection of the Beloved Son: The Transformation of Child Sacrifice in Judaism and Christianity* (New Haven, Conn.: Yale University Press, 1993) 181. He starts ch. 14, "The Rewritten Aqedah of Jewish Tradition," by commenting: "The extraordinary prominence of the story of the binding of Isaac in Gen 22:1-19 in rabbinic Judaism stands in stark contrast to the utter absence of direct references to it anywhere else in the Hebrew Bible. In part, the difference reflects the greater emphasis upon the Patriarchs in rabbinic theology than in the thinking of the prophets and the other non-Pentateuchal biblical authors" (173). He starts the whole book by affirming the importance of his theme for Jewish-Christian dialogue: "Radically transformed but never uprooted, the sacrifice of the first-born son constitutes a strange and usually overlooked bond between Judaism and Christianity and thus a major but unexplored

focus for Jewish-Christian dialogue" (x). He sees "Jesus' identity as sacrificial victim" to be more important than his Jewishness, but he concludes that it leads to supersessionism and "mutually exclusive traditions" (211), "a rivalry of two siblings for their father's unique blessing" (232).

[20] On the distinction between trust and belief see Martin Buber, *Two Types of Faith: A Study of the Interpenetration of Judaism and Christianity,* trans. Norman P. Goldhawk (New York: Harper & Row, 1961; originally published by Macmillan, 1951) 7–12, 170–4. However, I do not agree that "Emunah" and "Pistis" so sharply differentiate Jewish and Christian faith. Even the Pauline version of Christian faith is based in a relationship of trust before it is a believing that something is true. See, for example, Gal 2:19-20.

[21] Neusner, *Rabbinic Judaism,* 122. On 120–8 he discusses *Genesis Rabbah,* a rabbinic commentary on Genesis, in relation to Israel's history. On 45 he refers to *zekhut* as "unearned grace."

[22] Ibid., 125. Shalom Spiegel, *The Last Trial: On the Legends and Lore of the Command to Abraham to Offer Isaac as a Sacrifice: The Akedah,* trans. Judah Goldin (Woodstock, Vt.: Jewish Lights Publishing, 1993; Hebrew original, 1950) 116, uses the language of merit: "The Akedah merit proclaims and promises that the very grace of the Fathers lies in this: the sum of the righteousness of the Fathers is there to add to and complete the reward of the sons who engage actively in Torah; and thereby redemption makes haste to come."

[23] Levenson, *The Death and Resurrection of the Beloved Son,* 139. Ch. 12, "Isaac Unbound," 125–42, is a brilliant exposition of the *aqedah.*

[24] Spiegel, *The Last Trial,* 72: "Accompanying every one of the sacrifices being offered *in this place* is the memory and good work of the one who came to bind and the one who came to be bound" (emphasis in original). He is commenting on the rightness and propriety of the Temple-service in Jerusalem based on Gen 22:14. "This place" is named "YHWH will see" and was identified with Jerusalem in 2 Chr 3:1 and with Mount Gerizim (Shechem) in the Samaritan tradition.

[25] Levenson, *The Death and Resurrection of the Beloved Son,* develops this in his treatment of the story of Joseph: "The story of Joseph is the most sustained and the most profound exploration in the Hebrew Bible of the problematics of chosenness, one of the central theological concepts not only of ancient Israel, but of rabbinic Judaism and Christianity as well" (154). He sees Joseph's story as one of transformation and legitimation, a sign of "the mysterious grace that encompasses the life of the beloved son" (167). But, more than grace alone, God works through the moral and intellectual mettle of the favored son. "Joseph succeeds because of God's favor, but God's favor comes to the man who, because of his mounting strength of character and self-knowledge, is able to put it to the proper use" (167–8).

[26] Levenson, *The Hebrew Bible,* 153 (emphasis in original).

[27] Buber, *Moses,* 101–9, interprets the metaphor of "eagles' wings" as imaging not so much the speed or strength of YHWH as his parental care for Israel. "Here YHWH is likened in His historical relationship with Israel to the eagle, who stirs up his nest and hovers hither and thither above it in order to teach his young how to fly. . . . The great eagle spreads out his wings over the nestlings; he takes up one of them, a shy or weary one, and bears it upon his pinions;

until it can at length dare the flight itself and follows the father in his mounting gyrations. Here we have election, deliverance and education; all in one" (102).

[28] Norbert Lohfink, *Option for the Poor: The Basic Principle of Liberation Theology in the Light of the Bible,* trans. Linda M. Maloney (N. Richland Hills, Tex.: BIBAL Press, 1987, 1995) 27–39.

[29] Ibid., 32–3.

[30] Ibid., 35.

[31] Ibid., 37–8. At the end of this chapter on the Exodus story, Lohfink appends some considerations on the origins of Israel and affirms in line with what was said above that a complex and diverse group of people who all shared an experience of poverty and oppression eventually came to accept the exodus experience as expressing their own experience. "There must then at some time have come a point at which the whole complex of groups which had gathered into the tribal farming society of 'Israel' perceived the previous history of the group that had come out of Egypt as their own and narrated it as the beginning of Israel as a whole. This can only be explained if all these people had had analogous experiences in the events of their past history, which this story of the Exodus from Egypt expressed better than any other" (40). He concludes that *this story,* the exodus of the poor to form a new society in contrast to the feudal Canaanite city-states and the colonial overlords of Egypt, should be at the center of all contemporary liberation movements. In an analogous way, this is what Jesus was trying to accomplish (ibid., 61–3).

[32] Jacob Neusner, *The Theology of the Oral Torah: Revealing the Justice of God* (Montreal: McGill-Queen's University Press, 1999) 63, in discussing the moral order of reward and punishment, refers to Abraham (at Gen 18:23-25) as an enduring pattern found elsewhere in Scripture of the precision of judgment commensurate to action. However, the measure of retribution is exactly proportionate to the sin, while the measure of reward greatly exceeds the contrary measure. Yehoshua Amir, "Measure for Measure in Talmudic Literature and in the Wisdom of Solomon," *Justice and Righteousness: Biblical Themes and Their Influence,* ed. Henning Graf Reventlow and Yair Hoffman (Sheffield: Sheffield Academic Press, 1992) 29–46, makes the same point about proportionate punishment and abundant reward while discussing the tractate *Sota* in both the Mishnah and the Tosefta (33–36). Buber, *Two Types of Faith,* 152–4, also discusses the relation between judgment and mercy in terms of the "*middot* of God" (measures), i.e., "the *middah* of judgment and the *middah* of compassion" referring to *Midrash Genesis Rabbah* xxi.6. "Yet—and this is the most important—they are not equal to one another in power: the *middah* of grace is the stronger. . . . Because this is so, the world is preserved; were it otherwise, it could not continue" (153).

[33] Cross, *From Epic to Canon,* 6–7, 11, 15–19. He comments to the point: "The whole design and motivation of the covenanted league was the establishment of mutual obligations. The notion of a *bĕrît,* 'covenant,' in the era of early Israel without the mutual bonds of kinship-in-law between Yahweh and Israel, and between the tribes of the league, is not merely unlikely; it runs counter to all we have learned of such societies" (17). Chapter 1, "Kinship and Covenant in Ancient Israel" 3–21, is a new essay for this volume. Janzen, *Old Testament Ethics,*

who advocates the "familial paradigm" as primary, affirms that "individual laws are merely instrumental in achieving and/or safeguarding an ethos of communal life structured along kinship lines" (63). The components of the familial paradigm are: (1) *life* that includes the ongoing family line; (2) *land* as the gift of God's hospitality; (3) *hospitality* as the extension of life and land to the "other," the stranger or alien, because of need; (4) *an ethic rooted in God's story,* i.e., a family guided solely by God's promised future (40–6). He concludes the book: "A narrative-canonical approach assumes that the story itself, extending through both Testaments, is the ethic" (210).

[34] John R. Donahue, "Biblical Perspectives on Justice," *The Faith That Does Justice: Examining the Christian Sources for Social Change,* ed. John C. Haughey (New York: Paulist Press, 1977) 69. See also his *What Does the Lord Require? A Bibliographical Essay on the Bible and Social Justice,* rev. and expanded (St. Louis: Institute of Jesuit Sources, 2000) 23–4, where he refers to his earlier description of justice but says it must now be supplemented by the view of Walsh, *The Mighty from Their Thrones,* which we will use below. Donahue's bibliographical essay offers a very useful summary of the biblical development and an ample bibliography.

[35] Katharine Doob Sakenfeld, *Faithfulness in Action: Loyalty in Biblical Perspective* (Philadelphia: Fortress Press, 1985) 132. On 131 she recapitulates the basic meaning of loyalty. See also 40–2 on the relationship between loyalty and covenant.

[36] Ibid., 49: "The expression 'abounding in loyalty' is used in the Old Testament only of God, never of human beings. It is especially this greatness of God's loyalty that distinguishes it from human loyalty, which is often by contrast characterized as frail or fickle. This distinction corresponds to the observation that in the Old Testament, human loyalty is never associated with forgiveness; only divine loyalty extends that far in its will to maintain relationship." She is commenting on Exodus 32–34 to demonstrate God's "forgiving loyalty" (47–9).

[37] Jon D. Levenson, *Sinai and Zion: An Entry into the Jewish Bible* (Minneapolis: Winston Press, 1985; San Francisco: Harper & Row, 1987) 45.

[38] Ernest W. Nicholson, *God and His People: Covenant and Theology in the Old Testament* (Oxford: Clarendon Press, 1986) 148. He reviews the scholarly discussion on covenant since Wellhausen and concludes that there has been a shift from "covenant as a cultic or religio-sociological institution to covenant purely as a theological and didactic analogy" (85). He also finds the analogies to Hittite and later Assyrian treaty forms to be superficial in resemblance and improbable in the period of the late monarchy. This is dependent on his thesis throughout the book that the full-blown covenant concept was a late arrival in Israel, probably beginning with Hosea (ca. 750), although "the demand for Israel's exclusive allegiance to Yahweh" probably had earlier origins. "In the indisputably ancient traditions of Yahweh's deliverance of Israel's ancestors from bondage in Egypt and of his victories on behalf of the tribes of Israel against their enemies during the early generations of Israel's emergence in Canaan, Yahweh was acknowledged to be the God who alone stood at the foundation and beginning of Israel" (202). The Mosaic Covenant is usually thought to be analogous to a suzerain-vassal treaty, i.e., the obligation of the vassal to his master, and the Abrahamic and Davidic Covenants to a royal grant treaty, i.e., the obligation of the master to his servant. On the functional difference between

the "obligatory" type and the "promissory" type, see Moshe Weinfeld, "The Covenant of Grant in the Old Testament and in the Ancient Near East," *Journal of the American Oriental Society* 90 (1970) 184–203.

[39] Norbert Lohfink, *The Covenant Never Revoked: Biblical Reflections on Christian-Jewish Dialogue,* trans. John J. Scullion (Mahwah, N.J.: Paulist Press, 1991) 21. He notes that there are other texts that speak of covenant in various ways but these texts along with other images all speak about "God's relationship to particular persons, to his people, or to the whole human race." Sakenfeld, *Faithfulness in Action,* 42, observes that "it is widely agreed that in Israel's own reflection there were two general models of covenant thinking, usually referred to as the Sinaitic (or Mosaic) and the Davidic." She develops these models in relation to the theme of "loyalty" (42–63) and then considers the exilic development as "God's new way" that demands adjustments in covenant thinking (64–76).

[40] Levenson, *Sinai and Zion,* 70–5, 209–17.

[41] Ibid., 207. On 187–8 he says that Zion is an heir to Sinai, but always subordinate to the voice of Moses. This is the burden of part 3: "The Manifold Relationships Between Sinai and Zion."

[42] Sakenfeld, *Faithfulness in Action,* 98: "For the individual member of the community, as for the people as a whole, Yahweh's loyalty experienced in forgiveness undergirds every other manifestation of that loyalty. Psalm 32 states the point succinctly . . ." (there follows a citation of vv. 1, 3, 5b, 10-11). Chapter 4, "Help in Need" (83–98), reviews the preponderance of biblical testimony in the Psalms around the themes of deliverance from enemies, protection, and forgiveness.

[43] Lohfink, *The Covenant Never Revoked,* 48. My text is indebted to his exposition of Jer 31:31-34 on pages 45–51.

[44] Levenson, *Sinai and Zion,* 53.

[45] Moshe Weinfeld, *Social Justice in Ancient Israel and in the Ancient Near East* (Jerusalem: Magnes Press; Minneapolis: Fortress Press, 1995) 8–23.

[46] Sakenfeld, *Faithfulness in Action,* 101–27, develops Israel's calling around these themes.

[47] Abraham J. Heschel, *The Prophets,* vol. I (Peabody, Mass.: Prince Press, 1962; HarperCollins, 1969) 210.

[48] Rabbi Irving Greenberg, "Judaism and Christianity: Their Respective Roles in the Strategy of Redemption," *Visions of the Other,* ed. Fisher, 9. In the same volume Rabbi David Hartman, "Judaism Encounters Christianity Anew," sees "the soul of the covenantal message" as the confirmation of humans in their limitations (76). "The covenant, therefore, signifies for me the re-establishment of the dignity of the concrete. It is the celebration of human finitude. It is the ability to love in spite of human limitations, to build meaning in the face of death, to affirm today without the certainty of tomorrow" (78).

[49] Nicholson, *God and His People,* 215–6 (emphasis in original).

[50] Sakenfeld, *Faithfulness in Action,* referring to Abraham Heschel's notion of "divine pathos," especially in Hosea, observes: "The one aspect of loyalty that is most difficult to appropriate in Hosea's reversal of the usual direction of God to Israel is that of helper to the needy, the situationally powerful to situationally dependent. But precisely by using loyalty in such a gratingly impossible way of

Israel toward God, Hosea lifts up before his hearers the pathos of God, the deep yearning of God for the people's response, the relevance to God of their response. The divine initiative and pleading echo with a mix of love, anger, and frustration which eddy and swirl in expression of the anguish of God" (116).

[51] Heschel, *The Prophets,* vol. I, 122, commenting on Jer 14:19-21. Sakenfeld, *Faithfulness in Action,* 46, commenting on Jer 16:1-13, especially v. 5, says: "Jeremiah 16 stands alone in all of the Old Testament in its direct pronouncement of the end of divine loyalty."

[52] Walsh, *The Mighty from Their Thrones,* 5. John Reumann, "Righteousness: (4) New Testament," *The Anchor Bible Dictionary,* vol. 5, ed. David Noel Freedman (New York: Doubleday, 1992) 749, observes: "A striking reading of the OT evidence is presented by Walsh (1987: esp. 171–173), who invokes the theories on Israel's origins by Mendenhall and Gottwald." On 171–3 Walsh gives a summary of the book. On the interaction and inseparability of *mišpāṭ* and *ṣedeq,* he comments: "*Mišpāṭ* without *ṣedeq* is, in the long run, unsustainable. *Ṣedeq* without *mišpāṭ* is inefficacious" (171).

[53] Reumann, "Righteousness" 748. J. J. Scullion, "Righteousness: (1) Old Testament," *The Anchor Bible Dictionary,* vol. 5, ed. David Noel Freedman (New York: Doubleday, 1992) asks in his conclusion: whose *ṣedeq/ṣĕdāqâ*? God's or Israel's? He answers: "The *ṣedeq/ṣĕdāqâ* of the community and the individual is comportment according to God's order in every area of life, in just and proper social order (justice to the helpless, the poor, the oppressed, the widow, the orphan, the resident alien), in legal procedure, in the ritual of worship, all effected by God's *ṣedeq/ṣĕdāqâ*" (736).

[54] Weinfeld, *Social Justice,* 5. On 181ff. he explores the idiom *mišpāṭ wĕṣĕdāqâ* as bearing a unique meaning that *ṣĕdāqâ* does not have by itself. He translates it as "righteous justice" and relates it to YHWH's actions at creation, the Exodus, and the messianic future, as well as to the liturgical pattern of creation-revelation-redemption. For a comprehensive listing of all the texts on *ṣedeq/ṣĕdāqâ,* see Ahuva Ho, *Ṣedeq and Ṣedaqah in the Hebrew Bible* (New York: Peter Lang, 1991). For a more brief review of texts that emphasizes parallels to *ḥesed* and *răḥamîm,* see Eliezer Berkovits, "The Biblical Meaning of Justice," *Judaism* 18 (1969) 188–209.

[55] Bruce V. Malchow, *Social Justice in the Hebrew Bible* (Collegeville: The Liturgical Press, 1996) 76–8, concludes that Israel provides a model of dialogue with its "three methods of accepting, adapting, and transforming" in relation to its Near Eastern neighbors. His book provides a helpful review of the textual developments centering around the issue of social justice, as does Pleins, *Social Visions.* The two authors differ over whether the book of Proverbs merely advocates charity on the part of the elite (Pleins) or goes beyond charity to a level of social justice (Malchow). On the book of Psalms, which contains the largest number of usages of *ṣedeq* (50 times) and *ṣĕdāqâ* (34 times) according to Ahuva Ho, see J. David Pleins, *The Psalms: Songs of Tragedy, Hope, and Justice* (Maryknoll, N.Y.: Orbis Books, 1993).

[56] Janzen, *Old Testament Ethics,* 154, 156.

[57] Yairah Amit, "The Jubilee Law: An Attempt at Instituting Social Justice," *Justice and Righteousness,* ed. Reventlow and Hoffman, 47–59. In the same volume, Christofer Frey, "The Impact of the Biblical Idea of Justice on Present Discussions

of Social Justice," 91–104, makes a strong case for "sophisticated social ethics" that influence and shape institutions if there is to be sustainable justice. Likewise, Pleins, *Social Visions,* in his chapter on "Law and Justice," comments: "Indeed, the major drawback to adopting a so-called prophetic critique, as is so popular in some circles today, is that the prophetic literature often fails to advocate the kinds of concrete mechanisms that would be necessary for the alleviation of poverty in society. Each of the bodies of Torah legislation examined in this chapter goes far beyond the prophetic literature in this regard" (78).

[58] Shmuel Ahituv, "Land and Justice," *Justice and Righteousness,* ed. Reventlow and Hoffman, 27–8.

[59] Levenson, *Sinai and Zion,* 120: "What is certain is that the expression of the idea of Jerusalem as a cosmic center, the navel of the world, is fuller and more developed in rabbinic literature than in the Hebrew Bible." He reviews biblical and rabbinic texts on Zion and the Temple and concludes: "The Temple and Mount Zion retain a central role in the rabbinic tradition until this very day" (179). Jewish tradition, he observes, did not spiritualize Zion, Jerusalem, or the land of Israel, but retained their literal, historical significance. He points to three important factors in the development of the rabbinic tradition: (1) prayer is seen as a form of sacrifice (cf. Ps 141:2); (2) the synagogue succeeds the Temple, the rabbi inherits the authority of the priest, and the family table replaces the altar (i.e., the levitical system continues in another form); (3) observance of Sabbath and study of Torah is a proleptic experience of the "world to come" when sacred time and sacred space become one in the meeting of heaven and earth on "the mountain of the Lord."

[60] Norbert Lohfink, "Covenant and Torah in the Pilgrimage of the Nations (The Book of Isaiah and Psalm 25)," *The God of Israel,* Lohfink and Zenger, 40.

[61] Ibid., 192. The authors comment that God's will is one with regard to salvation (cf. Isa 66:18-23) but that the primary concern in the Bible is not the salvation of individual souls but the transformation of this world: "It is about the question of whether and how God succeeds in changing this human history, so deeply marked by guilt, discord, and violence, into that which God actually had in mind at creation. It is about the question of whether harmonious songs of praise can sound again from God's creation, whether in the desecrated and empty spaces of this world God's honor can be present again. At least that is the biblical form of the question of salvation" (196–7).

[62] Lohfink, *Option for the Poor,* 49–53.

[63] This text raises the oft-disputed question of the identity of the servant. Lohfink sees "all Israel as the poor of Yahweh." Pleins, *Social Visions,* 266, agrees: "Through the experience of judgment for its sin and rebellion, the *nation* has become *ʿānî*"(emphasis in original). He also raises the question of whether there might not be a shift from the more direct economic and political concern of Isaiah 1–39 to a concern of "the elite" about its own predicament and crisis of faith in exile. However, rather than viewing the elite as co-opting the image, their concern might help to explain the tension and ambiguity about the identity of the servant. Would the elite be able to accept an identification with the poor and suffering? "'There is no peace' *[šālôm]*, says the LORD, 'for the wicked'" (Isa 48:22; 57:21). In any event, including Third Isaiah in his analysis

(Isaiah 56–66), Pleins concludes: "The overall thrust of the prophet's message is that YHWH meets the chosen people in the midst of their suffering, affliction, and oppression. Just as YHWH sought out a people who were exploited in Egypt and led them out of that captivity, so YHWH seeks out those who are ensnared by circumstances beyond their control, exiles in foreign Babylon" (269). Further: "after the agony and suffering of the exile, the whole community came to understand the meaning of the *ʿānî* experience," and so is ready "to build a new and just national order" (270).

[64] Lohfink, *Option for the Poor,* 58. My exposition of Second Isaiah is indebted to his treatment on 53–8. Richard J. Clifford, *Fair Spoken and Persuading: An Interpretation of Second Isaiah* (New York: Paulist Press, 1984), sees the theme of Second Isaiah to be the necessity of returning to Zion, a new exodus and conquest, for Israel to be authentically Israel.

[65] Erich Zenger, in Lohfink and Zenger, *The God of Israel,* 161–90, analyzes Psalms 90–106 as also giving evidence of a greater turning once again to YHWH alone who in his great loyalty *(ḥesed)* will realize the *mišpāṭ* and *ṣĕdāqâ* given to Moses as a universal reign of peace and justice for the whole of creation.

[66] Lohfink, *Theology of the Pentateuch,* 173–226. Lohfink maintains a distinction between "a priestly historical narrative (p^g)" and the later "legislative priestly material (p^S)" (98, n. 5). He says that p^g "can be clearly distinguished both from the old sources of the Pentateuch and also from priestly legal material that was added later: it is an originally independent document" (119). An extensive development of his view with detailed text references is on 145–9.

[67] Ibid., 105–15. This is part of chapter 4 entitled "Original Sins in the Priestly Historical Narrative," 96–115.

[68] Lohfink develops these ideas in ibid., chapter 1, "'Subdue the Earth' (Genesis 1:28)," 1–17, and chapter 5, "God the Creator and the Stability of Heaven and Earth: The Old Testament on the Connection between Creation and Salvation," 116–35.

[69] Ibid., 210.

[70] Lohfink, "The Concept of 'Covenant' in Biblical Theology," *The God of Israel,* Lohfink and Zenger, 11–31, presents the canonical connections of *tôrâ* (23–5) as an argument against covenant being the dominant category in the Scriptures of Israel. However, he actually argues that, at least in the deuteronomistic perspective that has greatly influenced the canon, Israel receives *tôrâ* in the context of covenant which ties Israel's experiences together, though not as a single or fully harmonious system: "Rather the canon, with its different systems of expression that are to be distinguished from one another all along the line, has been put together to address a specific unified situation. It is meant to address post-exilic Judaism awaiting the coming reign of God" (29). This is certainly the situation in which Malachi writes.

[71] Pleins, *Social Visions,* 408, concludes: "Paganism may present challenges, but the ethical voice of the Mosaic covenant under prophetic mediation becomes a locus for the community to refine its ritual and reassert its commitment to the laborers, widows, orphans, and strangers." And further: "While Malachi marks the end of the book of the Twelve, the end of classical prophecy, and for Christians the terminus of the Old Testament, it is clear that this little

CHAPTER THREE

"*Strive First for the Kingdom of God and His Righteousness*" (*Matt 6:33*)

Jesus' Mission to Israel

"Thus says the LORD: maintain justice *[mišpāṭ]*, and do what is right *[ṣĕdāqâ]*, for soon my salvation will come, and my deliverance *[wĕṣidqātî]* be revealed" (Isa 56:1). The context of Jesus' life and times was a continuing experience of exile because of the successive rule of foreign powers culminating in the Roman imperial power.[1] Clearly, the hopes and expectations of first-century Palestinian Jews, be they Judeans, Galileans, or Samaritans, centered around the divine judgment *(mišpāṭ)* as vindication for the just and vengeance upon the wicked *(nāqām)*.[2] But, as with Malachi (3:18), God's judgment is not concerned primarily with the overthrow of foreign imperial powers, but with who is righteous and who is wicked within Israel. On a popular level, there were surely a variety of ways to imagine God's victory over the Roman Empire, whether through an apocalyptic cataclysm or via a warrior hero, perhaps an anointed one from the house of David, who would lead Israel in a holy war against the Romans.[3] But Jesus rejected these views (cf. Luke 17:20-21) in favor of Israel's integrity as a people that had accepted YHWH's *ṣedeq* and as such could be a light to the nations. Walsh comments: "It is against this background of expectation, flowing from the sense of *ṣedeq* and the belief in Yahweh's *mišpāṭ* found in the Scriptures, that Jesus is to be understood."[4]

Jesus himself might be bemused, if not befuddled, by the attempts of contemporary scholars to characterize him in his historical *persona*.[5]

William Herzog proposes as a hypothesis to be tested that Jesus was "a prophet of the justice of the reign of God." The conclusion to his discussion on prophecy and Jesus as prophet is worth quoting at length:

> Jesus was a popular prophet whose roots were deeply embedded in Galilean village life. He most likely came from a peasant artisan family and shared the values of village life while being familiar with its customs and traditions. Put differently, Jesus was a peasant prophet who interpreted the Torah not as a representative of the great tradition emanating from Jerusalem but as one who embodied the little tradition found in the villages and countryside of Galilee. At the same time, as a popular prophetic figure, he attracted crowds because he embodied the yearnings of the villagers of Galilee, who were increasingly separated from their land and traditions by an alien network of Roman domination, Herodian exploitation, and temple control. Insofar as he interpreted the Torah and argued its meaning, he was a prophet in the tradition of the Deuteronomist, a prophet who continued the paradigmatic work of Moses, the prototypical prophet. Insofar as he interpreted the social, economic, and political situation in the light of the covenant promises of Yahweh, he stood in the tradition of the great oracular prophets of Israel's past. Add to this mix Jesus' own distinctive voice, rooted in his reputation as a traditional teacher and healer, and the foundation is laid for understanding Jesus as prophet. The rest of this study will test this proposal.[6]

This seems a fair description of the sociopolitical context of Jesus and the way he would have been perceived by his contemporaries. The most important features are that he was a Galilean peasant,[7] a first-century Mediterranean Jew who lived in an honor-shame, patron-client agrarian society,[8] a rural villager who experienced the alienation caused by Roman imperial power, Herodian machinations, and the wealthy elite associated with the Temple aristocracy. As a religious Jew, his experience was shaped by the covenantal pattern of election and obedience to Torah.[9] Most importantly for our purposes, unlike his near-contemporary Hillel (60 B.C.E.–20 C.E.?),[10] Jesus did not interpret Torah in the manner of *halakhah* (a close reading of Torah to interpret and apply it to everyday life) but in the manner of *aggadah* (a narrative discourse that breaks Torah open to new possibilities, be they apocalyptic or socially transforming). Yet it can be maintained that neither Hillel nor Jesus correspond to later rabbinic tradition.[11] Indeed, unlike the purely didactic use of parables as illustrations to teach a moral found in the rabbinic tradition,[12] Jesus' parables are stories that have metaphoric impact, i.e., function like metaphors in identifying the narrative with perceived reality ("the reign of God is a man who had two sons . . .") and so serving to challenge assumptions and offer a new or alternative vision of the way things are.[13]

The question of who Jesus is only comes into clear and explicit focus in the light of his death and resurrection. In Bultmann's famous phrase, the proclaimer became the one proclaimed. For Jesus in his historical mission, the primary concern and focus was not himself but the reign of God and the justice that is integral to it (Matt 6:33 = Luke 12:31; cf. Luke 9:57-62 = Matt 8:19-22). As we said at the end of Chapter 1, the focal and key issue in the days of Jesus is not Christology but theology. Was Jesus right about God and especially about God's call for a renewal of covenantal fidelity and justice, i.e., for a renewal or revitalization of Israel? There are a variety of ways by which one might approach an answer to that question. In this book, we are following the methodological approach that proposes a particular hypothesis to be tested by the data, which may then demand a revision of the original hypothesis. The whole must be seen in terms of its parts and the parts in relation to the whole; this in preference to a piecemeal assembly of data with no connection to a larger whole.[14]

Our hypothesis is that Jesus was deeply imbued with the sense of justice found in the Hebrew Bible as we developed it in Chapter 2; i.e., that his aim or purpose can be understood in terms of the three questions for which we sought answers: (1) what makes Israel free: liberation from exile; (2) what constitutes Israel as Israel: covenantal fidelity and justice; (3) what gives Israel a future: YHWH's return to Zion. This is a schema, but it is new in that I am not aware of anyone who has tried to make a point by point correlation between a coherent and self-contained vision of justice as found in the Hebrew Bible and Jesus' historical mission. Obviously, Jesus addressed these issues within the concrete social and cultural conditions of his time and with his own unique style and emphasis. Hence, without pretending to give an exhaustive treatment of what might be said about Jesus in his historical mission, we will examine this hypothesis under the heading of the four key points adumbrated at the end of Chapter 2.

YHWH Alone Is King in Israel

Jesus never refers directly to YHWH as king (cf. Psalms 93; 95–99). He prefers the less common expression kingdom or reign of heaven. But his proclamation of the kingdom's arrival (Mark 1:15) is an announcement of victory (*euangelion:* good news) that only God can bring (Mark 1:14b) because, as in the Exodus experience, YHWH is the only one who can free the people from their exile. Mark recognizes this by invoking the promise of Malachi (3:1) and Isaiah (40:3) at the beginning of his Gospel (1:2-3). What Jesus announces is the consolation of YHWH, the divine initiative that requires a human response.[15] As with Second

Isaiah, this is already a call to be released from exile and to return to Zion.[16] There are no limits to what YHWH can do, because "for God all things are possible" (Mark 10:27).[17]

YHWH's liberating initiative in no way depends on the mediation of other power brokers, certainly not Caesar, not Herod, not the wealthy elite associated with Temple hegemony. For Jesus, the only mediation of God's initiative on the human side is the power of love and service. Central to his teaching was the heart of the Torah: *šĕmaʿ yisrāʾēl* ("Hear, O Israel!" at Deut 6:4), that affirms the uniqueness of YHWH and the command to love YHWH with one's entire being. Mark employs a concentric structure that parallels a synthetic saying about love of God *and* love of neighbor (Mark 12:28-31), with an antithetical saying about "paying back" *(apodote)* or "rendering service" to Caesar *or* to God (Mark 12:13-17). The "way of God" (v. 14) is not the way of Caesar. If you bear the image *(eikōn)* and name *(epigraphē)* of Caesar (v. 16), then you are indebted to him and the system he represents.[18]

These two sayings surround the central dispute with the Sadducees concerning the resurrection. Basing their argument on Mosaic law (v. 19 = Deut 25:5), Jesus in turn appeals to the power of God and to Moses' experience of God (Exod 3:6), a God indeed of the living and not of the dead. These sayings have been brought together in Mark 12 as part of a series of controversies following upon the Temple incident. But, in doing so, Mark has brought out a central feature of Jesus' historical mission: everything is related to YHWH, the God of Israel, as revealed in the Torah of Moses. There may be disagreements with his fellow Israelites about interpretation, but it is interpretation about YHWH who is the only king in Israel and whose kingdom has "drawn near" (*ēngiken:* Mark 1:15). In this kingdom, there is no place for the oppressive imperial power of Caesar.

Nor of Herod, who wanted nothing so much as to win the favor of Caesar. The one direct reference to Herod on the lips of Jesus is decidedly not complimentary ("that fox" at Luke 13:32). Jesus ignores the cities founded by Herod, Sepphoris, and Tiberias (named after Caesar), probably because Herod's attempts to establish them as administrative centers of an elite market economy ran counter to the kinship ideals of the Torah and the prophets (cf. Neh 5:1-11) and so to Jesus' vision of shared goods in communal village life. "In such conditions the reciprocal system of exchange with its inbuilt concerns for all members of the extended household or clan is more favourable to the poor than is the market economy which functions in favour of the ruling elite and to a lesser extent their administrative retainers."[19]

Finally, while Jesus could effectively ignore or avoid the Roman imperial power and the Herodian ruling elite, he would eventually have to engage the wealthy elite associated with Temple hegemony if his vision of God's reign was to survive in a lasting way. We will discuss the significance of his final actions in Jerusalem later under the rubric of YHWH's return to Zion, but for the moment we need to look at his attitude toward the Temple and its practices as it touches his understanding of the God of Israel. Zion, i.e., Jerusalem and specifically the Temple mount, is (or should be) the dwelling place of YHWH. There is no clear evidence that Jesus thought otherwise. The accusation at his trial that he would destroy the Temple is ambiguous and conflicting (Mark 14:58-59; note the variant forms at Matt 26:61 and John 2:19, and its absence in Luke). The explicit prediction of the Temple's destruction (Mark 13:1-2 par.) pertains to the actual event in 70 C.E. Luke-Acts makes the Temple thematic for the life of Jesus (especially Luke 1–2 and 24:44-53) and for the beginning of the Christian community (Acts 1–5; cf. 21:15-26). However historical these accounts may be, it is hard to imagine that Luke would have employed this theme if Jesus himself had clearly denigrated the Temple as such. Luke does follow Mark in including the prediction of the Temple's destruction at 21:5-6, but this pertains to a narrative time much later than his narrative of Jesus and the early community. There are indications that Jesus had no problem with the normal functions of the Temple if they correspond to the law of Moses: he tells the cured leper to go to the priest and to make the appropriate offering according to the command of Moses (Mark 1:44 par.; cf. Luke 17:14); he tells Peter to pay the Temple tax even though the children are free (Matt 17:24-27); he assumes the legitimacy of offering gifts at the altar even though reconciliation takes precedence (Matt 5:23-24). Indeed, if he has a criticism, it is not against the Temple as such but against practices that lead to neglect of "the weightier matters of the law" (Matt 23:23 = Luke 11:42).

The three terms in Matthew can be understood from the Hebrew Bible as *mišpāṭ (krisis), ḥesed* (*eleos;* cf. Hos 6:6), and *ʾĕmûnâ (pistis)*. But tithing according to Leviticus 27:30-33 (cf. Mal 3:8-10) is still to be observed. The parallel at Luke 11:42 has "justice *[krisis]* and the love of God." The scribe's response to Jesus' declaration of the two greatest commandments as love of God and love of neighbor (only at Mark 12:32-34), that these commandments are "much more important than all whole burnt offerings and sacrifices," is in line with the prophetic critique that views the worship of YHWH (cultic or ritual *tôrâ*) as inseparable from the service of YHWH in the neighbor (ethical or social *tôrâ*), both of which are necessary to maintain the covenant (cf. Isa 1:10-17; Jer 7:1-7; Hos 6:6; Amos 5:21-24; Mic 6:6-8; Mal 3:1-5). Jesus declares that the scribe is "not far from the kingdom of God."

Jesus' concern, from first to last, was to move the stubborn and deeply-rooted intransigence of the human heart. "For truly I tell you, if you have faith the size of a mustard seed, you will say to this mountain, 'Move from here to there,' and it will move; and nothing will be impossible for you" (Matt 17:20). "This mountain" refers not just to any mountain but to a particular mountain, the Temple mount, which as the place where YHWH dwells cannot tolerate oppression of the alien, the orphan, and the widow, the shedding of innocent blood, the practice of idolatry, the robbing of the poor (Jer 7:1-15; Mark 11:17 par.).[20] Nothing is impossible for one who has faith, for God, for Jesus' Abba.

YHWH's ṣĕdāqâ: *Renewal of Covenantal Loyalty*

What did Jesus hope to accomplish? "The synoptic Jesus lived as a law-abiding Jew."[21] Yet it is also true to say that he was a man of Spirit who "sought the transformation of his own social world."[22] These two statements, both of which are true, must be held in tensive unity. What startled Jesus' contemporaries was his power/authority *(exousia)* manifest in both his teaching and his healing (Mark 1:27 sees the two activities as inseparable). Matthew characteristically schematizes Jesus' activity as teaching, preaching, and healing: "Jesus went throughout Galilee, teaching *[didaskōn]* in their synagogues and proclaiming *[kērussōn]* the good news of the kingdom and curing *[therapeuōn]* every disease and every sickness among the people" (Matt 4:23; cf. 9:35; 11:1). We will take a brief look at each of these activities through the lens of his call to renew covenantal loyalty, recognizing at the same time that the offense and opposition he caused stemmed primarily from his claim to be acting with the power and authority of God's spirit.[23]

Jesus' proclamation of the good news of the kingdom calls for a radical response. It will be recalled that the notion of *ṣĕdāqâ* in the Hebrew Bible includes YHWH's creative vision for a new world order that must be embraced and shared by those whom he has chosen (e.g., Abraham at Gen 15:6 and "all the people" at Exod 24:3, 7-8). This is the covenant in blood, a communal/corporate embodiment ("con-sensus") of covenantal loyalty that alone can sustain YHWH's *mišpāṭ*. When Jesus announces that the kingdom of God has drawn near, he calls for a communal response: "repent, and believe in the good news" (Mark 1:15). Underlying the Greek imperatives in the second person plural *(metanoeite kai pisteuete)* would be the Hebrew understanding of *šûb*, i.e., a radical "turning" *(teshuvah)* or change of mind and heart that involves the whole person/community, and of *ʾĕmûnâ*, i.e., not simply believing that Jesus' word is true but a complete and total entrusting of oneself as a member of the community to this vision of God's victory. Jesus' proclamation entailed an unremitting concentration on the one thing necessary, the kingdom of God (Matt 6:25-34 = Luke 12:22-32; Luke 9:60b, 62). But what exactly was his vision of God's kingdom? To answer that we turn to the new and inclusive possibilities for the communal life of Israel manifest in his healings, his meals, and his teaching in parables. Then, in the next section, we will ask how his vision took shape in the structures that constituted Israel's identity: Torah, land, and kinship.

"Healing is the restoration of meaning to life."[24] John Pilch, in his analysis of the healing stories in the four Gospels, emphasizes the difference in cultural context between modern medicine that seeks to *cure* a *disease* (the scientific and empirical analysis of a loss of function and the attempt—rarely successful—to find a cure) and traditional cultures that seek to *heal* an *illness* (the attempt, especially of folk healers, to restore someone who is experiencing a disvalued state of being to a context of meaning within the community—usually successful). One particularly clear example is leprosy. Modern medicine has analyzed it as Hansen's disease. In the Bible (Leviticus 13–14) it is an illness, a condition of uncleanness that forces the leper out of the community not for reasons of contagion (which assumes modern knowledge of bacteria and viruses) but for reasons of pollution. To say that Jesus cured the disease of leprosy is anachronistic and ethnocentric. It is a failure to employ a cross-cultural hermeneutic.[25] In reference to the story of the leper at Mark 1:40-45, Pilch comments:

> The afflicted one (leper) requests Jesus to "make him clean" and Jesus obliges. He says: "I will [it]; be [made] clean!" The theological passive voice indicates that God is the agent who cleansed the afflicted ones. Jesus declared the petitioner clean, that is, acceptable and welcome in the community. Jesus extended the boundaries of society and included in the holy community many who were otherwise excluded (lepers, tax collectors, prostitutes).[26]

Jesus' healings and exorcisms signal the arrival of God's kingdom, of God alive, active, and present in a way that demands a reconsideration of where the threat to the community's holiness (Lev 19:2b) truly lies, that is, within the community and particularly in hardness of heart (Mark 7:6b, 21-23; cf. Mark 6:52; 8:17-18 in reference to the disciples). Jesus' compassion (Mark 1:41; in Greek, *splangchnistheis;* in Hebrew, *răḥamîm*) moves him to touch and be touched by the excluded and so reinstate them within the community. In the honor/shame culture of Jesus' day, the "poor" are those who are unable to maintain their social standing.[27] As Bruce Malina notes, the meaning of "poor" will vary, depending on whether one is politically unable (oppressed), economically unable (indigent), kinship unable (outcast/sick), or religiously unable (ignorant). The key is the sense of belonging rooted in kinship. Jesus in his practice of healing challenges the politically embedded religion of Israel with a renewed sense of belonging based on forgiveness and faith.

The forgiveness of sins is connected to the forgiveness of debts (Matt 6:12; cf. Luke 11:4), to whatever has brought shame or dishonor to the person. "Forgiveness thus has the character of restoration, a return to both self-sufficiency and one's place in the community."[28] Faith as it would have been used by Jesus, in the sense of *ʾĕmûnâ,* is a matter of communal/covenantal loyalty. In the story of the paralytic, Jesus connects *their* faith (Mark 2:5 par.) with such forgiveness. In the similar story at John 5:2-9 the man is without kinship support (v. 7), but in the subsequent action of the story he does seek to reinstate himself with the dominant group (v. 15). Both are necessary: the restoration of honor (forgiveness) and the sense of belonging to the covenantal community (faith). In the account of the paralytic, Jesus declares forgiveness by using the divine passive *(aphientai),* so why do the scribes complain of blasphemy because only God can forgive sins (Mark 2:7 = Luke 5:21; Matt 9:3 includes the charge of blasphemy but omits the question)? Herzog sees this healing as a challenge to the Temple or at least to those who would claim that only the priestly sacrificial system can broker God's forgiveness.[29] At least Jesus sees that his mission (to paraphrase v. 10: "a man like myself," that is, I myself and anyone who has been given the same mission from the Father) includes the authority *(exousia)* to declare God's forgiveness. The clincher, of course, is that the man is healed and can go home on his own power. But what is crucial for rural peasants, if they are to keep the covenant, is not so much the sacrificial system as forgiveness and loyalty, love and service. Central to these covenantal virtues is hospitality, as seen in the case of the woman who bathed Jesus' feet with her tears and wiped them with her hair (Luke 7:36-50) in contrast to Simon who shows no hospitality (vv. 44-46). Jesus identifies her action of service to him with great love and healing faith, so that her many sins are forgiven.

This woman, like the woman bound by Satan for eighteen long years and set free on the sabbath, was also "a daughter of Abraham" (Luke 13:16). Indeed, all of Jesus' healings can be understood as a restoration of the person to the community. One thinks, for example, of Simon's mother-in-law who serves the disciples (Mark 1:29-31 par.), of the leper whose observance of Mosaic law (Lev 13:49; 14:2-32) would be "a testimony to them" (Mark 1:44 par.), of the paralytic who "went out before all of them" (Mark 2:12 par.), of the man with the withered hand who was given new life on the sabbath (Mark 3:1-6 par.), of the woman who had been suffering from hemorrhages for twelve years and who told the whole truth in the midst of the crowd (Mark 5:25-34), and the girl intertwined with the story of the woman as she died at the age of twelve (Mark 5:21-24, 35-43) who was restored to the family table (v. 43b). Whether the word "faith" is explicitly used or not, the principle that all things are possible for one who believes (Mark 9:23) is operative. Interestingly, Jesus pushes the boundaries of covenantal fidelity when he attributes faith to the Samaritan leper (Luke 17:19), to the Canaanite woman (Matt 15:28), and to the Roman centurion (Matt 8:10 = Luke 7:9). But, as we have seen, the fate of Torah has implications for the Gentile world. Jesus senses, however inchoately, that there are possibilities beyond his own mission to the lost sheep of the house of Israel (Matt 15:24; cf. Matt 8:11 = Luke 13:29).

Of all of Jesus' healings the most significant were his exorcisms, for here he directly confronts the power of Satan with the power of the Spirit given to him and here he meets the greatest opposition, not only from the demons themselves but also from those who question his authority *(exousia)*. In responding to the charge that he casts out demons by Beelzebul, the prince of demons (Mark 3:22 par.; Matt 9:34), Jesus again affirms the arrival of the kingdom: "But if it is by the finger of God that I cast out demons, then the kingdom of God has come to you" (Luke 11:20 = Matt 12:28, which reads "by the Spirit of God"). To the more insidious charge that he is possessed by Beelzebul (only at Mark 3:22, 30; cf. John 7:20; 8:48, 52; 10:20), he responds that "blasphemy against the Spirit will not be forgiven" (Matt 12:31b; Mark 3:29 [v. 30 connects it to the charge of possession]; Luke 12:10 = Matt 12:32). This does not refer to some unimaginable sin outside the reach of divine forgiveness but to the very specific situation of Jesus' claim to be announcing and effectively enacting God's reign with the power and authority of God's Spirit. This calls for a response of "turning" and "trusting" in absolute obedience to God's Spirit. Those who refuse are missing the decisive time (*kairos:* Mark 1:15), the fulfillment of God's promises to Israel.

Among those who, at least initially, responded to Jesus' preaching and healing were the marginalized, the "toll collectors and sinners." Jesus was not only their friend; he even ate with them (Mark 2:14-17 par.; Matt 11:19 = Luke 7:34; Luke 15:1-2). Sharing table, which meant sharing in God's blessing, was a powerful symbolic enactment of the kingdom and especially of God's blessing upon the "poor." It was another way by which Jesus restored those who had lost honor to their rightful place in the community. He was extending hospitality to those who might be considered strangers or even enemies, i.e., a threat to the holiness and purity of Israel. In doing so, he was simply fulfilling the teaching *(tôrâ)* of Moses that includes not only neighbor and resident alien (Lev 19:2b, 9-10, 18, 33-34) but also an enemy or "one who hates you" (Exod 23:4-5). Jesus by this prophetic action challenged any practice of sharing meals that would be exclusive.[30]

That he wished to include everyone—masters and servants, patrons and clients, rich and poor—in a renewed communal vision of the agrarian society of his day is, it seems to me, the main point of his teaching in parables. What is impossible for the rich still remains possible for God (Mark 10:27 par.). Unlike an allegorical interpretation that tells us what God is like or a moralistic interpretation that looks for an ethical application, Jesus' parables identify God's reign with the social conditions and experiences of his people, which were his own experiences, so as to give shape to a new or alternative vision of that same reality. "Historically speaking, Jesus sought to transform his social world by creating an alternative community structured around compassion."[31] This is true above all of his parabolic teaching.

How does Jesus accomplish this? In a number of parables that focus on the social dynamics of power, he presents rich and powerful men as heroes who act in ways diametrically opposed to cultural expectations. For example, a patriarchal father filled with compassion embraces his wayward son who had treated him as if he were already dead (Luke 15:11b-32), a rich businessman praises his unjust steward (Luke 16:1b-8a), a vineyard owner pays indigent day-laborers, even the last who only worked one hour, enough to survive for another day (Matt 20:1b-14a), an absentee landlord risks sending his only son in the face of murderous tenants who had already dishonored him (Mark 12:1b-8). In another reversal, a despised and hated Samaritan, taking the place of an Israelite as hero, shows extraordinary compassion to an enemy (Luke 10:30b-35). Thus, God's reign includes not only wayward sons, unjust managers, poverty-stricken day-laborers, desperate tenants who even resort to murder, and hated Samaritans, but also patriarchal fathers, rich businessmen, employers who possess the earth's resources, absentee landlords who demand rents, and Israelites who should show compassion even to hated enemies.

The kingdom of God is indeed in the midst of the people (Luke 17:21). In his teaching, parabolic and otherwise, Jesus talks about the *realities* of peasant life: poverty, indebtedness, hunger, sickness (especially demon possession), patriarchal structures, rulers (patrons, masters) and ruled (clients, servants), taxation systems, and agrarian life such as crop failures compared to rich and abundant harvests (Mark 4:3-8 par.; cf. 4:26-29, 30-32).[32] What he is saying is that things could be different and that Israel is called by God to embody that difference. This is what the covenant means. When he says, "Blessed are you poor, for yours is the kingdom of God" (Luke 6:20), he is not saying that it is good to be poor, not politically, not economically, not religiously, and certainly not as an outcast with no kinship support. Neither is he saying that the poor are somehow more virtuous than the rich. What he is saying is that God is alive, active, and present as the only one who rules, as the only legitimate patron, calling the community to covenant loyalty, i.e., to change the conditions that create divisions between rich and poor, master and servant, patron and client. This demands on the part of rich and poor alike a profound "turning" of mind and heart and a willingness to "entrust" the collective self to this good news of God.

Two parables found only in Luke (18:2-5 and 18:10-14a, omitting the redactional introductions and conclusions), one concerning the practice of the courts and the other prayer in the Temple, illustrate what is at stake in terms of justice *(mišpāṭ)* and righteousness *(ṣĕdāqâ)*.[33] In the case of the judge and the widow, Jesus presents a judge who respects neither the God who gives the Torah nor the people whom Torah is supposed to benefit. He is a corrupt judge who renders verdicts in favor of the wealthy elite. They pay him to keep the system in their favor. The widow whom God promises to protect as he did the people in Egypt (Exod 22:21-24) breaks through the conspiracy of silence and the vulnerability of her position as a woman without a male protector. She demands that the judge do right to her *(ekdikēson me)*, i.e., that he give her the justice Torah demands, and he finally does so lest she give him a black eye *(hypōpiazē me)*, the final ironic word of the parable. Thus, she breaks through the collusion of an oppressive system: "The refusal of the widow to accept her predestined role breaks social barriers and crosses forbidden social and gender boundaries. The result of her shameless behavior is a just verdict."[34]

The second parable, the Pharisee and the toll-collector in the Temple, is similarly the story of a man, despised and rejected as a deviant, who refuses to be silenced by the system, in this case a system that labels him as an extortioner, swindler, and adulterer (v. 11) who has no place in the Temple precincts and should leave in silence,

> a shamed man put in his place. But he does not go quietly. Having heard the worst that the Pharisee could throw at him, he cries out, beats his breast, and prays for mercy, the very mercy being made available through the afternoon sacrifice. He refuses to consent to the Pharisee's shaming but appeals to a higher source. He refuses to accept the labels attached to him, the stigma of toll collector, but speaks directly to God, seeking mercy. He breaks the deafening silence that followed the Pharisee's effort to reinforce the status quo. He breaks through the intimidation and fear that the Pharisee's words have created, and by his actions, he challenges the Pharisee's reading of God's judgments.[35]

Even more strikingly, he makes a direct claim upon God, as should every Israelite since God alone is ruler and patron, that God make an atonement for him (v. 14: *hilasthēti* connotes atonement specifically rather than mercy in general). It is a bold prayer, but his utter reliance upon God alone, like Abraham at Genesis 15:6, enables him to participate in YHWH's *ṣĕdāqâ*.

In this section, we have been describing Jesus' activity of preaching, healing, sharing meals, and teaching as calling Israel to a renewal of covenantal loyalty through a "turning" and a "trusting" that will enable the people, especially the rural peasants, to embody YHWH's *ṣĕdāqâ*. To discover the reign of God, the people must not look away from their lives and their communal relationships but more deeply into them (Luke 17:21; Mark 1:15). God's reign includes liberation from the power of evil (Luke 11:20 = Matt 12:28; Luke 7:22-23 = Matt 11:4-6). Above all, it includes those who have been excluded and marginated but who are now breaking out of their enclosure and pursuing/grasping what Jesus is talking about (Matt 11:12; cf. Luke 16:16; 6:20).[36] However, Jesus' mission was not just to inspire or instruct, but to embody the will of God in specific structures. He was "the master builder of the house of God."[37]

YHWH's **mišpāṭ**: *Reconstitution of Israel*

To be effective, YHWH's and Israel's *ṣĕdāqâ* must take the concrete and specific shape of YHWH's *mišpāṭ*. Israel survived the desolating experience of exile, the loss of monarchy and Temple, because it had the *tôrâ* of Moses. Thus, the question of who belongs to the kingdom of God is not finally dependent on those particular structures in their limited, historical manifestations, but it must take some structural form. Given the fluid and shifting nature of Jesus' ministry,[38] not to mention its brevity (two to three years?) and its consummation in failure on the cross, the structures he created and/or advocated would not have been fully developed and would have been reshaped after his death and resurrection. Nonetheless, contrary to those who would portray Jesus as "a structureless, radical egalitarian,"[39] as some sort of cynic critical of and opposed to all forms of organization and authority, we maintain that Jesus, as a first-century Palestinian Jew closely connected to the traditions of his ancestors, and especially to the *tôrâ* of Moses as embodying the *mišpāṭ* of YHWH, would naturally and necessarily look to create or re-create some structures. Otherwise he would have been inept and ineffective, if not downright foolish, and so easily ignored. In this section we will view this proposal under the lens of Torah, Land, and Kinship. In the final section, we will focus on the Temple.

In the context of his people's hope that YHWH would deliver Israel from her continuing exile, "Jesus saw his prophetic mission as one of regathering the scattered twelve tribes of Israel in the end time and of preparing this reconstituted Israel for God's coming in power to bring

Israel's history of salvation to completion."[40] For this to happen, the fundamental and indispensable condition is the fate of Torah in Israel, i.e., Israel must become a just society (Isa 1:16-17, 21; 2:2-4; 5:7; Mic 4:1-4). When Jesus interprets Torah, two things must be kept in mind. First, he does not teach in the manner of rabbinic *halakhah,* i.e., he does not give specific rulings on the application of the law.[41] As noted in connection with his teaching in parables, he speaks from experience, the concretely lived experience of his contemporaries, rural, Jewish, Galilean, because it was his own experience. He is thus primarily interested in the intent of Torah as life-giving within the actual conditions of first-century Palestine. Second, his aim is not to abolish or abrogate Torah but to bring even the smallest letter and seemingly most insignificant stroke or accent mark to the fullness that God has intended for heaven and earth, for the whole of creation (Matt 5:18; cf. Luke 16:17). Thus, his aim is not to abolish but to interpret (Matt 5:17) the whole Torah as a matter of God's "righteousness" (Matt 5:20).[42] His interpretations are in the spirit of Jeremiah 31:33: "But this is the covenant that I will make with the house of Israel after those days, says the LORD: I will put my law *[tôrātî]* within them, and I will write it on their hearts; and I will be their God, and they shall be my people." Jesus appeals both to the God who has written the divine law according to the original intention of the Creator from the very beginning (e.g., Mark 10:6-8 = Matt 19:4-5; citing Gen 1:27; 2:24) and to the human heart as precisely the place where God writes and humans accept or reject the divine justice (e.g., Mark 7:21 = Matt 15:19; cf. Isa 29:13-14).

This is the way we should read the most famous compilation of Jesus' interpretation of the law, the six "antitheses" found in Matthew 5:21-48.[43] It has been common to treat the sayings on murder, adultery, and love of neighbor as confirming the deeper intent of the law and the sayings on divorce, oaths, and retaliation as abrogating specific laws. The antithetical form with the Greek *de* is not strongly adversative and the formulation may not come from Jesus as it is found only in Matthew. In any event, all six of the sayings can be read as a deepening of the intent of the law that has both antecedents in the Hebrew Bible and in the differing interpretations of Jesus' contemporaries.

In the first antithesis, Jesus is clearly affirming the commandment not to kill, but he is also drawing upon the proverbial wisdom (frequent in the book of Proverbs) that anger, an interior attitude of heart and mind, can and does have devastating consequences, especially if it issues in insulting and abusive language. Matthew connects this with two independent sayings about reconciliation (5:23-26) that bring out his understanding of the intent of Jesus. There is no doubt that Jesus valued reconciliation, especially through forgiveness that restores one's place within the community, but the focus of the saying as given (5:21-22) is upon "judgment" (*krisis*, i.e., *mišpāṭ*). Deuteronomy (16:18-20) speaks of judges and officials appointed for the tribes who must render "just decisions" *(mišpāṭ-ṣedeq)* for the people (v. 18). "Justice, and only justice *[ṣedeq ṣedeq]*, you shall pursue, so that you may live and occupy the land that the LORD your God is giving you" (v. 20). Jesus understands this justice to extend to the attitudes of heart and mind if Israel is to be ready for the coming kingdom.

In the second antithesis, Jesus in the same manner is affirming the commandment against adultery while drawing upon both biblical and popular wisdom with regard to looking that can turn to lust (think only of the story of David and Bathsheba). Matthew again connects this to independent sayings about the consequences of giving in to temptation (5:29-30; cf. 18:8-9; Mark 9:43-48). But the focus of the saying as given (5:27-28) is upon male attitudes toward "a woman" (whether married or betrothed). In addition, the tenth commandment, "you shall not covet . . ." (Exod 20:17), is the only commandment not able to be judged by external criteria. The phrase at Matthew 5:28, *pros to epithumēsai* = "with lust," could be translated: "in order to covet . . ." (cf. Rom 7:7 where Paul uses the same word, translated as "You shall not covet"). Thus, Jesus is reinforcing the tenth commandment with respect to coveting "your neighbor's wife."

The second antithesis is closely allied to the third as both deal with male treatment of women. In Jewish society only a husband could divorce a wife (though a wife could appeal to a tribunal to force the husband to initiate divorce proceedings). Deuteronomy 24:1-4 is case law concerned about a particular problem: can a divorced wife return to her first husband if her second husband also divorces her? The answer is no, but the law does envisage at least the possibility of divorce. It certainly does not encourage the practice. Later rabbinic disputes, notably between the house of Hillel and the house of Shammai, focused upon the cause since the phrase at Deuteronomy 24:1, translated as "something objectionable about her," is very ambiguous. The question at Matthew 19:3 ("for any cause") and the exceptive clause at Matt 5:32 and 19:9 (using *porneia*, the meaning of which is also highly disputed) probably reflect this rabbinic debate.[44] Both the question at Mark 10:2 ("Is it lawful for a man to divorce his wife?") and the first half of the antithesis at Matt 5:31 ("Whoever divorces his wife, let him give her a certificate of divorce") place the focus not upon the reasons but upon the practice. The first half of the response at 5:32 (minus the exception) is striking: "But I say to you that anyone who divorces his wife . . . causes her to commit adultery" (or "makes her an adulteress": *poiei autēn moicheuthēnai*). In the other versions, it is always the case of divorcing and marrying another (Matt 5:32b; 19:9; Luke 16:18; Mark 10:11-12; Rom 7:3). But how does the simple fact of being divorced make the woman an adulteress?

In Jesus' day, men defended the honor of the family to the outside world while women defended the honor of the family by maintaining a sense of shame (a positive virtue) within the household. A divorced woman without a male protector would be seen as shameless and vulnerable to male advances. The sin of adultery was understood as primarily a matter of honor between males. One male dishonors another who in the person of his wife has not protected his honor and the honor of his family. Women were vulnerable in this system. That is why widows (along with orphans and strangers) are singled out for YHWH's special protection. Jesus extends this protection to women facing the possibility of divorce by focusing upon the responsibility of the male in causing the oppression of a divorced wife. Her options were few: return to her father's house (unlikely), find another husband (possible, but not too likely),[45] live without a male protector in terrible vulnerability (very likely). Thus, Moses allowed divorce because of "hardness of heart" (Mark 10:3-5 = Matt 19:7-8), but from the beginning of creation it was not so. Jesus, for his part, recognizes what the law says but challenges the practice as demeaning to women. This coheres well with his public inclusion of women in the ongoing process of the kingdom's arrival.

The fourth antithesis does not seem to be aimed at swearing falsely by the name of YHWH (Lev 19:12) or at taking an oath in a strictly judicial setting, but at oaths (or vows) freely made to God which should be kept (Num 30:2; Deut 23:21-23). One can also refrain from vows and, presumably, oaths (Deut 23:22). Jesus' response is aimed at the common practice of pronouncing an oath to verify one's word, e.g., the price of something for sale in the market, while avoiding the Name, as in "by heaven," "by the earth," "by Jerusalem," or by the hairs on one's head (cf. the similar criticism at Matt 23:16-22). The arrival of the kingdom depends upon a community where people say simply and directly what they mean without equivocation or subterfuge. Sophistic or hypocritical oaths come from the evil one; the simple and unadorned truth from the Spirit (cf. John 14:17, 26; 15:26; 16:8-11, 13).

Similarly, the fifth antithesis recognizes what the law permits (retaliation but under strict control: Exod 21:23-24; Lev 24:19-20; Deut 19:21). Jesus' response focuses not upon the legitimacy of the law as such, which was after all concerned to control through legal means the strong urge for unlimited revenge, but upon perceived injustice. When he says do not resist or stand up to evil or the evildoer, he is not saying do not resist evil. He spent his whole life resisting the power of evil. But he is saying do not resist evil with evil (cf. Rom 12:17-21). The examples adduced cover a range of everyday experiences: insults, injustice in a lawsuit, forced conscription, neighbors in need (cf. Luke 6:29-30). The last is simply a call to observe the law as found in Leviticus 25:35-38 and Deuteronomy 15:7-11. The latter concludes (v. 11): "Since there will never cease to be some in need on the earth, I therefore command you, 'Open your hand to the poor and needy neighbor in your land.'" In this spirit, Jesus says elsewhere: "For you always have the poor with you, and you can show kindness to them whenever you wish" (Mark 14:7; cf. Matt 26:11; John 12:8; both of which omit the latter phrase). Once again, as with divorce and oaths, Jesus is not abrogating the law but interpreting it in a way that will make a renewed Israel ready for the coming kingdom.

The final saying about helping a needy neighbor (v. 42), even if there be conflict because the neighbor is viewed as an evildoer, leads into the sixth antithesis that makes the point even more emphatically. The law never says that one should hate one's enemies, so this would appear to be a popular interpretation. The law does say: "you shall love your neighbor as yourself" (Lev 19:18) *and* "you shall love the alien as yourself" (Lev 19:34). Jesus extends the law to include everyone, and especially the enemy and persecutor, so that the Israelites may truly be children of the Creator God who sends sun and rain on evil and good, just and unjust alike. In this he again invokes his basic principle of interpretation: the creative intention of God from the beginning. For Jesus, fulfilling the *tôrâ* of Moses in this way will make Israel "perfect" (v. 48: *teleios;* cf. Matt 19:21), i.e., fully what God intended Israel to be from the beginning.

In conclusion, Jesus' teaching is that the whole Torah should be fulfilled in ways that are life-giving. YHWH's *mišpāṭ* includes attitudes and actions toward a brother, a married woman, a divorced woman, as well as a readiness to speak the truth on all occasions, to respond to perceived injustice with good rather than evil, and above all to love even the enemy. One could adduce other examples, but this is sufficient to show that Jesus sought to renew Israel by calling all the people to a faithful observance *(ṣĕdāqâ)* of what God has decreed *(mišpāṭ)*. The God of Abraham, Isaac, and Jacob is God of the living. This God calls Israel to be a just society.

The second lens for viewing Jesus' intent regarding structures is the Land. Central to the Exodus experience is the promise of the land that YHWH gives to all the people because both land and people belong to YHWH. The Torah certainly legitimates the Temple and the priesthood, as is evidenced in the "holiness code" (Leviticus 17–26) and throughout the Pentateuch, but always within the context of YHWH's free and gracious creation of his own people who recognize YHWH alone as their king. It is YHWH's holiness that makes the people holy (Lev 19:2b). It is

YHWH's promise of the land that is their inheritance (Num 26:52-56; Josh 13:1–21:45; Ezek 47:13–48:29). As Naboth tells Ahab: "The LORD forbid that I should give you my ancestral inheritance" (1 Kgs 21:3). Who inherits the land? Those who are humbly obedient (Matt 5:5), those who hunger and thirst for God's justice (Matt 5:6).[46] Obedience to Torah, to YHWH's *mišpāṭ*, demands that *all* the people (rich and poor alike) share in the abundant fruitfulness of the land. It is not necessary to hold that Jesus was trying to separate Temple from land as Herzog maintains—after all, Zion was the center of Israel's post-exilic hopes—to affirm that he was challenging the domination systems of his day.

There are two things that Jesus emphasizes in this regard: the freedom that comes to those who trust in God alone and the belonging that comes to those whose debts are forgiven. Both are necessary for a renewed Israel. The first involves a communal sense ("con-sensus") of complete trust in the news of God's victory. The sayings of Jesus collected at Matt 6:25-34 (= Luke 12:22-32) remind Israel (the verbs are all in the plural) of the God who gives life. If the birds of the air and the lilies of the field, then how much more you, O Israel, who unlike the nations (*ta ethnē:* Matt 6:32 = Luke 12:30) have been given the kingdom (Luke at 12:32 adds the saying about the "little flock": *to mikron poimnion*). Relying on God alone (cf. Luke 18:9-14) means overcoming fear and seeking the one thing necessary: the justice of God's reign. This includes an attitude of service to one another rather than of claiming to be the first or the greatest (Mark 9:34-35) and of "lording it" over others (Mark 10:42-44 par.). In a renewed Israel of the coming kingdom, the first will be last and the last first, the exalted will be humbled and the humbled will be exalted, and the greatest will be the servants of all, for in Israel all are children of God (Matt 18:3-4) and claim equal inheritance. The parables of land and seed can also be understood as a call to trust and to persevere in the face of failure and even of oppressive systems of domination. The three parables at Mark 4:3-9, 26-29, 30-32 all celebrate the fruitfulness and abundance of land and seed as coming from God and embodying what God's reign is all about. But, insofar as these parables point to failure, resistance, and oppression, they also call for a human response to God's gift of life in the form of forgiveness and reconciliation that will transform society into God's *šālôm*.

The issue that is of greatest structural significance is the forgiveness of debts in the spirit of the jubilee law at Leviticus 25:10ff. The law was intended to prevent economic inequality, exploitation, and domination and to create a different society. It is dependent not upon ruling authorities (king or priest) but upon God. Debt means the loss of land and often leads to slavery. But this land and this people are not to be enslaved by alien powers for they belong to God alone. Hence, in the prayer that Jesus gives to his disciples, the petitions for bread and for forgiveness of debts ask God for that which is necessary right here and now in the present crisis.[47] That the crisis is signally one of loss of land and consequent indebtedness is reflected in the subject-matter of many of the parables: day-laborers (Matt 20:1b-14a) who, homeless and landless, are the most indigent; tenants (Mark 12:1b-8) who, having lost their inherited land, must work for absentee landlords; a manager (Luke 16:1b-8a) who resorts to cheating in order to survive; a destitute beggar (Luke 16:19-26) whom a rich man cannot see even though he is at his gate. Finally, in an interesting reading of the story of the rich man at Mark 10:17-22,[48] Herzog maintains that the commandments left out (no gods but YHWH, no idols, no wrongful use of the Name, sabbath observance, and no coveting) are precisely the ones that the rich, by reason of their greed, have not kept. He distinguishes between purity codes in the Torah that preserve the community from pollution (e.g., Deut 22:9-11) and debt codes that call for a redistribution of the land's resources (e.g., Lev 25:23-55). He concludes:

> Quite clearly, the rich man had a robust conscience bolstered by his reading of the Torah and supported by his daily effort to root out impurity and so avoid the contagion of pollution. This is why Jesus must restate the import of the Decalogue in a startling way. All ten commandments can be viewed as an expression of the debt system. They provide different points of entry into the world of the covenant and its demands for justice in the land. But the rich ruler has read them through the demand for purity, and as a result he can no longer perceive the great injustice at the heart of the purity codes. . . . The four commandments, go, sell (dispossess), give (distribute), and follow me, summarize Jesus' reading of the Decalogue as seen through its debt codes.[49]

This is to read the Torah "as God intended the Torah to be," i.e., as a demand for justice in the distribution of the land so that all Israel may "inherit eternal life" (Mark 10:17), the kingdom of God.

Turning to the third lens regarding structures, namely Kinship, it is important to stress that Jesus, as with the rich man, exhorts a wide range of people to follow him. The radical urgency of Jesus' call and the intense concentration on the one thing necessary, God's reign and his righteousness (Matt 6:33), are brought out clearly in the three sayings on following Jesus at Luke 9:57-62 (Matt 8:18-22 parallels the first two sayings with some modifications). In the first, a man (Matthew has a scribe who addresses Jesus as "teacher") says to Jesus, "I will follow you wherever you go," and Jesus replies that "a man like myself" (the Son of Man) has nowhere to lay his head. Jesus surely accepted the hospitality of others (e.g., Mark 1:29 par.; Luke 7:36; 10:38; Mark 14:3 par.), encouraged his disciples to do the same on their mission (Mark 6:10 par.), and may even have had a home of his own (Mark 2:1). However, his reply to the one who would follow him anywhere is that anyone who has the same mission that he has ("a man like myself") will experience risk and insecurity, even to the point of not having a place to call one's own. In the second saying, to another whom Jesus calls to follow him (Matthew specifies him as already a disciple) and who asks to first go and bury his father, Jesus replies with the most abrupt and startling saying in the tradition: "Let the dead bury their own dead" (Matthew prefaces it with the exhortation "follow me"; Luke appends, "but as for you, go and proclaim the kingdom of God").

Martin Hengel has taken this saying as a paradigm for all of the texts that signal Jesus' call to follow him. Its distinctiveness guarantees its historicity. "There is hardly one logion of Jesus which more sharply runs counter to law, piety, and custom."[50] E. P. Sanders, following Hengel's lead, sees it "as being the most revealing passage in the synoptics for penetrating to Jesus' view of the law, next only to the conflict over the temple."[51] He insists that both question and answer refer to a real situation that must take into account not only the positive call to discipleship but also "the negative thrust: Jesus *consciously* requires disobedience of a commandment understood by all Jews to have been given by God."[52] Sanders is surely correct that the negative impact of the response is what gives the saying its effectiveness. However, because of his skepticism about the historical veracity of the sayings of Jesus,[53] he isolates this logion too much. It is effective precisely as a hyperbolic statement about the primary importance of the mission. Of itself, it makes little or no sense. It must be seen in connection with other sayings about the family (Mark 3:31-35 par.; Luke 11:27-28, 52-53 par.; 14:26 par.; 18:28-30 par.) and balanced by Jesus' affirmation of the commandment to honor father and mother (Mark 7:10-12 par.; 10:19 par.). In particular, when Jesus says, "Whoever does the will of God is my brother and sister and mother" (Mark 3:35 par.), he is speaking to fellow Israelites and calling them to that will of God which is inseparable from *tôrâ,* from what constitutes Israel precisely as *kin*. But this does imply a distinction within Israel itself of those who do (the just) and do not do (the sinners) the will of God. This may be the import of the third saying (Luke 9:61-62) about not looking back. The decisive time of the mission is also a time of judgment.

Jesus' call to follow him is not, we are suggesting, without structural import. It is not a naked and serendipitous call to go where no one has gone before. It is a call for a renewal of the communal life of Israel. The expectation of the endtime, far from precluding any interest in forming structures or leadership groups, demanded it. We see this at

Qumran and in the movement that survived the death of John the Baptist. A structureless, egalitarian band of wandering cynics would have made no sense in the context of the eschatological expectations of Jesus' Jewish contemporaries. John Meier, in making this point, refers to an "embryonic structure created by Jesus during his own ministry." He distinguishes between "supporters" (Martha and Mary, Lazarus, Zacchaeus, Peter's mother-in-law), who stayed within the confines of village life to offer hospitality in various ways, and "followers," which includes the crowds in a rather fluid and unstable sense but refers specifically to disciples, those whom Jesus summoned to follow him on his itinerant mission and so to share in all the dangers, hostilities, and privations that would come with the mission. From among the disciples, then, Jesus chose "the Twelve" to form an innermost circle and to symbolize the re-gathering of the twelve tribes in order to restore Israel at the endtime. In the tradition of prophetic action, Jesus "was not only symbolizing but actually setting in motion the ingathering of all Israel in the end time."[54]

Such an ingathering assumes a return to the ideals of the Exodus experience, including the tribal league, as a "contrast society" in which there are no more poor and oppressed. One of the roles that Jesus assigns to the Twelve is to sit on twelve thrones judging the twelve tribes of Israel (Matt 19:28c = Luke 22:30b).[55] What would be the basis of that judgment if not Israel's response to Jesus' mission? "The Israelites themselves will be judged by whether they have eliminated poverty in Israel by following Jesus and acting accordingly."[56] Though specified now by the message of Jesus, this call to judgment is in the spirit of Isaiah:

> The LORD enters into judgment *[bĕmišpāṭ]* with the elders and princes of his people: It is you who have devoured the vineyard; the spoil of the poor is in your houses. What do you mean by crushing my people, by grinding the face of the poor *[ʿăniyyîm]*? says the Lord GOD [YHWH] of hosts (Isa 3:14).

Inseparable from the judgment that Jesus announces is his call of "sinners" (Mark 2:17 par.) and the salvation of a "remnant" (Luke 12:32).[57]

One of the key contributions of E. P. Sanders in his book on Jesus is his treatment of "sinners." Terminologically, he distinguishes sinners as the "wicked" *(rĕšaʾîm),* those who reject the law (covenant) and do not repent; the "people of the land" *(ʿammē ha-ʾāreṣ̂),* the common people whose lack of education and non-observance of purity laws would not exclude them from salvation; others like the *ḥaberim* who voluntarily maintained themselves in a relatively high state of ritual purity, the Pharisees who were exact and accurate interpreters of the law, and the *ḥakamim* who were the learned (by rabbinic standards). The real issue, says Sanders, is what it would have meant to offer the kingdom to the *wicked:*

> I propose, then, that the novelty and offence of Jesus' message was that the wicked who heeded him would be included in the kingdom even though they did not repent as it was universally understood—that is, even though they did not make restitution, sacrifice, and turn to obedience to the law.[58]

He correctly concludes that Jesus did not call sinners to repent as normally understood, but to accept him and his message. But that message *was* a call to repentance, not in the specific sense of making restitution to an offended neighbor and/or the appropriate sacrifice to God in the Temple (though I do not think Jesus excluded such observance of the law), but in the more fundamental sense of a radical turning and entrusting (Mark 1:15 as analyzed above) that would constitute a renewed vision of Israel. Sanders stresses the lack of a call to repentance as a return to Torah (many authors think that John the Baptist was calling for a return to Torah but not Jesus) and the striking inclusion of the "wicked," but he never mentions this inclusion as a challenge to the rich and powerful who consider themselves to be the righteous. Mark 2:17 could be understood to be just such a challenge.

David Flusser maintains that by Jesus' day the traditional division between just and sinner was breaking down. His statement of the traditional view is worth quoting at some length:

> The religion of Israel stressed the existence of one righteous God; his iconoclastic exclusiveness was linked with his inflexible moral will. The righteousness of the Old Testament seeks concrete expression in a new and just social order. God's righteousness is also his compassion; he espouses especially the cause of the poor and oppressed. He does not desire other people's physical power and strength, but their fear of him. The Jewish religion is a religion of morality in which the principle of justice is indispensable. That is why the division of human beings into just and sinners is so important. For the Jew, the concept that God rewards the just and punishes the wicked is the confirmation of God's steadfast truth. How, otherwise, could the righteousness of God prevail in the world?[59]

His point is that life refutes the view that the righteous flourish and the evil come to a bad end. In the second century B.C.E. this new sensitivity was in evidence. For example, the Wisdom of Jesus son of Sirach, notably conservative in his view of observance of Torah, stresses forgiveness, overcoming of anger to receive healing, mercy to receive mercy, setting aside of enmity (28:2-6), and concludes (v. 7): "Remember the commandments, and do not be angry with your neighbor; remember the covenant of the Most High, and overlook faults." Flusser maintains that Jesus radicalizes forgiveness and mercy in his exhortation to love one's enemy. As the sun rises on both righteous and unrighteous, so God's kingdom comes to sinner and righteous alike. Jesus' inclusion of sinners is meant to break down a wall of hostility and prejudice and to establish the kingdom on a radically inclusive forgiveness and merciful love *(ḥesed)*. This means that no member of the community of Israel, bound together by kinship ties, should be denied covenant status.[60] This woman, bound by Satan for eighteen long years, is a daughter of Abraham (Luke 13:16).

Yet judgment must surely come, for without judgment there can be no justice. "Jesus could not preach the reign of God without speaking of judgment."[61] And judgment implies that, however open and inclusive the original invitation, not all will respond.[62] Reiser sees the emphasis of John the Baptist upon judgment and of Jesus upon salvation as two sides of the same coin. "But while the Baptizer sets the impending judgment in the foreground of his preaching and shows the way to avoid it [by being baptized], Jesus gives pride of place to the present and future salvation [by announcing the kingdom], and shows the consequences of rejecting it."[63] In my view, both John and Jesus appeal to the "whole of Israel" but also recognize that only a few, a "remnant," will respond. Reiser differentiates between the judgment of Israel and the judgment of individuals, but the texts employed clearly refer to both as one cannot separate individuals from the community. In any case, he concludes that Jesus' preaching to both the nation and individuals is clear and consistent: repent in the sense of accepting his message and doing what he says. In his chapter on "the judgment of Israel," Reiser provides a convincing analysis of the following texts: the Queen of the south and the Ninevites (Matt 12:41-42 = Luke 11:31-32), the woe over the Galilean cities (Matt 11:21-24 = Luke 10:13-15), the saying about Abraham, Isaac, and Jacob in the reign of God (Matt 8:11-12 = Luke 13:28-29), the parable of the futile invitation to the feast (Luke 14:16-24 = Matt 22:2-14 = Thomas, logion 64), the slain Galileans and those struck by a tower (Luke 13:1-5), the saying on the harvest and laborers (Matt 9:37 = Luke 10:2; cf. Matt 10:14 par.; Mark 4:29), and the Twelve as judges of the twelve tribes (Matt 19:28 = Luke 22:28-30).

In an excursus on repentance, Reiser comments: "While for the Baptizer repentance still meant turning back to the Torah, and thus received its concrete content from the Torah itself, Jesus' idea of repentance was turning to him and his message; it is this message, then, that supplies the content of the repentance he demands."[64] But what precisely is the content of that message? Is it a simple call to repent and do penance according to the demands of Torah? Is it a call to repent in the face of the imminent arrival of the kingdom (inseparably connected to the person of Jesus) so that, at the last judgment, "the message will take the place of the Torah"?[65] We have been suggesting throughout a third alternative: that his message was about a radical change of heart and mind *(metanoia)* which includes the key elements of forgiveness of debts, faithfulness *(ʾĕmûnâ)*, and loyalty *(ḥesed)* to the covenant expressed in the *tôrâ* of Moses. The first three sayings listed above set up a contrast between Israel and the Gentiles to the disadvantage of Israel, but, as Reiser notes, they show Jesus' concern for Israel, his desire to shake the people up and get them to think and respond. The fact that Jesus does turn to words of judgment probably reflects his largely unsuccessful activity in Galilee as his ministry there was coming to an end. The only recourse was to set his face toward Jerusalem (Luke 9:51).

YHWH's Return to Zion: Judgment and Restoration

It is unimaginable that Jesus would not have seen Jerusalem as the center of Israel's hopes and so of his own as well. He never uses the terms "Zion" or "the Land," but he does speak of Jerusalem as "the city of the great King" (Matt 5:35), as the city where prophets die (Luke 13:33), as the city where YHWH as mother hen has often desired to gather her children (Luke 13:34 = Matt 23:37), and as the city that by its refusal is now forsaken and desolate (Jer 22:5) and so will not see YHWH until it says, "Blessed is the one who comes in the name of the LORD" (Ps 118:26; Luke 13:35 = Matt 23:38-39).[66] He surely knew the tradition of YHWH's desire to restore Jerusalem to the eschatological glory promised to her as the mother of Israel (e.g., Isa 54:1, 6-8; 66:7-9, 10-11, 12-14). But he also knew that the restoration or regathering of Zion was inseparable from the divine judgment (Isa 1:21-31; 3:1ff.; 4:2-6; 5:7; 65:1-16, 17-25; Jer 7:1-11; 29:10-14; 30:1–31:40; Ezek 16:1-63).

Jeremiah 22:3-5 is typical and catches well the intention of Jesus:

> Thus says the LORD: Act with justice and righteousness *[mišpāṭ wĕṣĕdāqâ]*, and deliver from the hand of the oppressor anyone who has been robbed. And do no wrong or violence to the alien, the orphan, and the widow, or shed innocent blood in this place. For if you will indeed obey this word, then through the gates of this house shall enter kings who sit on the throne of David, riding in chariots and on horses, they, and their servants, and their people. But if you will not heed these words, I swear by myself, says the LORD, that this house shall become a desolation.

Why will Jerusalem, "the great city," suffer desolation and destruction? "Because they abandoned the covenant of the LORD their God" (Jer 22:8-9).

Jesus did not come to Jerusalem to foment rebellion, nor did he come to die, but he did come to challenge Jerusalem to live out in covenantal loyalty YHWH's vision *(ṣĕdāqâ)* of justice *(mišpāṭ)*. The strength of Kim Huat Tan's book lies in showing that Jesus appropriated Zion's hopes and expectations in a creative way and so acted from a unified motivation and with a definite purpose. To demonstrate how, he proposes that the three actions of entry, Temple, and final meal exhibit an underlying unity, which he characterizes as a "restoration thread"; i.e., the three actions are unified around the eschatological fulfillment of YHWH's restorative blessings.[67] Focusing on the actions at this point and bracketing the controversy and eschatological discourses, we will consider the three scenes in sequence, following the accounts in Mark as the most reliable historically.

Mark's account of Jesus' entry into Jerusalem (Mark 11:1-10 par.) indicates that Jesus' action was deliberate as the planned arrangement for the animal (vv. 1-6) and the provocative posture of riding it (v. 7) make manifest. As Tan puts it, the crux of understanding this action is that it was a planned event, that it cannot be understood apart from the other two actions, and that as a symbolic action it required no commentary from Jesus. Both Matt 21:4-5 and John 12:15-16 see it as fulfilling Zech 9:9. Jesus does not cite this text; he *enacts* it in order, as Tan says, to signal the reign of God, God's promises of the restoration of Jerusalem, coming to fulfillment as a reign of peace. Both Sanders and Tan see this symbolic action as indicating a central role for Jesus as the "humbly obedient" king (Zech 9:9) who "comes in the name of the LORD" (Ps 118:26).[68] Although the implications of these biblical texts may not have been immediately obvious to the crowd and/or disciples (cf. John 12:16), they can help us to understand the intention of Jesus.

Psalm 118 is the last of the "Egyptian Hallel" Psalms (113–118) which praise the Lord *(halĕlu-yāh)* principally for his steadfast love *(ḥesed)* and faithfulness *(ʾemet)*, which endures forever (e.g., Ps 117). Psalm 118 is a psalm of thanksgiving that begins (vv. 1-4) and ends (v. 29) with the phrase, "his steadfast love endures forever." The psalm centers around the theme of rejection, even to the point of death (vv. 17-18), reversed by YHWH's salvation/vindication (vv. 14-16, 21-24). The use of this theme citing verses 22-23 at Mark 12:10-11 par.; Acts 4:11; 1 Peter 2:7 reflects the experience of Jesus' death and resurrection, but surely has its basis in Jesus' experience of the rejection of his mission and the expectation that God will vindicate his mission and message (and so, at least implicitly, his own role in that mission). Jesus' entry into Jerusalem is a petition to be admitted at the Temple gates: "Open to me the gates of righteousness *[ṣedeq]*, that I may enter through them and give thanks to the LORD" (v. 19). "This is the gate of the LORD; the righteous *[ṣaddîqîm]* shall enter through it" (v. 20) is the response from within the Temple. Mark 11:9 cites verse 25: "Save us" *[hōšîʿānnâ]* and verse 26a: "Blessed is the one who comes in the name of the LORD." The other evangelists make the christological implications explicit (Matt 21:9 = "the son of David"; Luke 19:38 = "the King"; John 12:13 = "the King of Israel"), but Mark (11:10) associates it with "the coming kingdom of our ancestor David." One can conclude from this that what Jesus expected was the divine vindication of his message of the kingdom at the Temple gates: "We bless you from the house of the LORD" (Ps 118:26b).

Yet there is a dark side to the joy of daughter Zion and the shouts of daughter Jerusalem (Zech 9:9) as they see their king coming, triumphant *[ṣaddîq]* and victorious *[nōšāʿ]*, for he is also humble *[ʿānî]*, which carries the connotation of being bent down or afflicted.[69] He comes to bring "peace to the nations" (v. 10) and the gathering of the dispersed has begun "because of the blood of my [YHWH's] covenant with you" (v. 11: *bĕdam-bĕrîtēk;* cf. Exod 24:8; Mark 14:24). Yet this ideal king associated with the house of David (12:7-8) may also be the one who was slain and over whom the house of David and the inhabitants of Jerusalem mourn as over a beloved child and a firstborn (12:10-14). In another image, the shepherd-king will be smitten and the sheep scattered (13:7-8), yet a remnant will be purified and saved in a renewed covenant (13:9). Through it all the final victory belongs to YHWH who "will become king over all the earth" (14:9). These images in Zechariah recall the pre-exilic Zephaniah's description of the people of Jerusalem as afflicted *[ʿānî]* and miserable *[dāl]* who, as "the remnant of Israel," seek refuge in YHWH (3:12-13). They also recall Second Isaiah's depiction of Israel in exile as poor and oppressed, but now as YHWH's servant who will teach justice to the nations (42:1-4), particularly by revealing as the suffering servant the violence and injustice of both the nations (50:4-11; 52:13-15) and Israel (53:1-9). The fate of Israel is inevitably tied to the fate of the suffering servant. However implicit and allusive (I doubt that Jesus ever formally referred to himself as the "suffering servant" or its equivalent), Jesus' action of entering Jerusalem and coming to the Temple moves in this direction. If our analysis has been correct so far, his intention in proclaiming the arrival of the kingdom has been to reconstitute Israel as a just society that includes the poor, the oppressed, and the marginated, so that at last Israel will have returned from exile to the land and the renown promised to the patriarchs, with YHWH enthroned in their midst (as envisioned in the later addition at Zeph 3:14-20).

When Jesus came into the Temple and looked around at everything (Mark 11:11a), what did he see? He did not see "a house of prayer for all the nations" (Isa 56:7) but rather "a den of robbers" (Jer 7:11). The full text as given at Mark 11:17 is integral to an adequate understanding of Jesus' actions. In this case, the citations are needed to make sense of the action. Isaiah 56:7 is the culminating statement of the opening of Third Isaiah (56–66), an author who affirms that all peoples are included in the new and glorious Jerusalem that YHWH, who alone redeems Zion, will create (60:1-22), but only if they "hold fast my covenant" (56:2, 4, 6) described in the opening verse as maintaining *mišpāṭ* and doing *ṣĕdāqâ*. "Thus says the LORD God, who gathers the outcast of Israel, I will gather others to them besides those already gathered" (56:8). This is what Jesus hoped to see, a vision of eschatological fulfillment in the place where YHWH dwells, a Temple prepared to receive all the nations. But Jesus, like Jeremiah, stands at "the gate of the LORD's house" (Jer 7:2) and recalls the word of YHWH:

> For if you truly amend your ways and your doings, if you truly act justly one with another, if you do not oppress the alien, the orphan, and the widow, or shed innocent blood in this place, and if you do not go after other gods to your own hurt, then I will dwell with you in this place, in the land that I gave of old to your ancestors forever and ever (7:5-7).

Thus, as Tan also argues, the meaning of Jesus' action in the Temple was not an attack symbolizing the destruction of the Temple while looking for its restoration at the eschaton, as Sanders argues, nor simply an act of symbolic cleansing or purification to prepare for its eschatological function in a renewed Zion, as many have argued, but a prophetic protest. Tan considers all *four* actions as given in Mark to have a unified and consistent significance. (1) Driving out "those who were selling and those who were buying" refers to merchants trading with the Temple staff, not to the common folk who gave Jesus popular support (as at Mark 11:18). (2) Overturning "the tables of money changers" challenges the corrupt and oppressive financial practices of the Temple aristocracy, including the system of taxation. (3) Overturning "the seats of those who sold doves," who, although representing the offering of the poor, were still subject to profiteering. (4) Not allowing anyone "to carry anything *[skeuos]* through the Temple," a puzzling reference that only Mark 11:16 has, probably referring to a sacred vessel used for carrying materials to be stored by the Temple staff and later sold to the populace as part of the profiteering. Thus, as Tan concludes: "Jesus was protesting against the temple establishment for turning the sacrificial system into an oppressive profit-making industry."[70]

Israel survived the loss of both monarchy and Temple during the exile because it had the covenant established at Sinai and specified in the *tōrā* of Moses. Jesus knew that. He also knew that the voice of Sinai was heard on Zion. The hope of Israel, symbolized as the reign of God, was meant to be realized at the symbolic center of Israel, the Temple on Mount Zion. The fact that Israel, embodied in its leaders, its priests and shepherds, was not yet ready to hear that voice meant that in the spirit of his protest he was called to create an alternative symbolic embodiment of a renewed or restored Israel. He did this by eating and drinking in an upper room on or near Mount Zion around the time of the Passover feast.[71]

There are a number of close connections between the last supper and the entry narrative, not the least of which is the mention of the kingdom (Mark 11:10 points to 14:25). As with the entry, the supper is a planned event as the prearranged upper room indicates (Mark 14:12-17 par.). There is a deliberately provocative, indeed shocking, action in the command to eat flesh and drink blood. There is the connection with Jerusalem and the Temple mount (Zion). There is the saying about the kingdom that evokes the hope of Israel's restoration and that is strategically placed by Mark as the climactic pronouncement of each scene. Both actions have a self-reference to Jesus' role in the coming kingdom, the first implicit and the second explicit. Both have their context of meaning in biblical texts that express the hope of divine vindication based on YHWH's faithful love (Psalm 118 in the entry and Exodus 24 in the meal). Both are, at least by implication, associated with Israel's fate as the suffering servant of YHWH (Mark's addition at 14:24b makes this explicit, as is already the case at Mark 10:45). Indeed the meal is surrounded with betrayal and the very real probability of imminent death (Mark 14:10-11, 18-21, 26ff.).[72] The saying at Mark 14:25, even as an independent logion, indicates that Jesus at some point saw the probability of his own death as *somehow* integral to God's intentions for the arrival of the kingdom. But the real *crux* of interpretation is what Jesus meant by referring to *his* "flesh" and the covenant in *his* "blood." The Aramaic word *bisrāʾ* is best translated as "flesh" (John 6:51 explicitly identifies the bread with flesh), and the idea of eating someone's flesh is a biblical metaphor for hostile action[73] (Ps 27:2; Zech 11:9; also Zech 11:4-14 portrays the rejection of a shepherd that has many resonances with the passion narratives). Jesus identifies his betrayer as "one of the twelve, one who is dipping [bread] into the [same] bowl with me" (Mark 14:20 par.). If Luke 22:19b-20 is taken as a later scribal addition modeled on 1 Corinthians 11:24b-25a,[74] then the end of verse 19a, "This is my body [flesh]," is immediately connected to verse 21, "But see, the one who betrays me is with me, and his hand is on the table." In any event, the saying about the bread as his flesh (body) means that he was experiencing a being "handed over" to death by those who reject and betray him (Mark 9:31a; 14:21, 41).[75]

But the real concern for Jesus at this moment is not so much whether or how he will die, nor even that he is being handed over by one of the twelve, but rather that "the Twelve" continue as symbolic of God's people, constituted as such by the covenant at Sinai and called to embody the fulfillment of God's promises. "We suggest that the failure of the temple to be the temple of the eschaton led Jesus to constitute definitively the restored people of God through a covenant-ratification ceremony so that this community would serve as recipients and bearers of God's eschatological blessings."[76] In my view, this community need not be understood as a new community replacing the old. Rather, it is the true fulfillment of YHWH's call to covenantal loyalty. Taking Meier's reconstruction of the authentic saying, "This cup is the covenant in my blood," the intent is to invoke the Sinaitic covenant at Exodus 24:8. All the traditions refer to the blood (Mark 14:24; Matt 26:28; Luke 22:20; 1 Cor 11:25; John 6:53-56), but only Paul (and Luke) to "the new covenant" (Jer 31:31, but blood is not mentioned). As Meier puts it: "The emphasis here seems to be not on the abrogation and replacement of the 'old' covenant by a 'new' one, but rather on the consummation or perfect fulfillment of the Sinai covenant at the climax of Israel's history."[77] Thus, Jesus' vision of YHWH's justice, rejected in Galilee and resisted in Jerusalem, takes an institutional form that is an alternative to the current corruption in the Temple (cf. the community at Qumran) and yet is in continuity with the priestly historical narrative (P^g as analyzed by Norbert Lohfink; cf. the end of Chapter 2). Jesus' response to the threat of violence against his life, to the slander against God's good gift embodied in his message of God's rule as a reenvisioning of Israel's deepest traditions, and to the refusal to turn and to trust in YHWH's power so as to honor YHWH alone as the only king in Israel, is to create a kind of "subsociety" around the Twelve that will continue to embody in both ritual and service (Luke 22:24-30 par.; John 13:1-5, 12-16) the covenantal ideals of the tribal league.

When he identifies the bread and the cup as "my flesh" and "my blood," he is at least implicitly identifying his destiny with the fate of Israel as the Suffering Servant. Mark 14:24b and Matthew 26:28b make the identification explicit in their elaboration of the cup word. As at the entry into Jerusalem, Jesus does not make the identification explicit verbally so much as he symbolically enacts it in a "covenant-ratification" ceremony. Thus, the corporate selfhood of Israel is identified with the despised "other" of Isaiah 52:13–53:12, the servant who reveals to the nations their iniquity, their violence, their injustice, and to Israel her true identity as YHWH's "poor" and her destiny as a light to the nations. "Yahweh is the god of *ʿapīru*."[78] The strange God of exodus who called Israel to be different among the nations, the merciful God of exile who called Israel to recognize a new identity as a light to the nations, is the same God of Jesus who continues to call Israel to follow the way of YHWH, to return at last from exile, so that all the nations may stream to Zion. The question for

Jews and Christians remains. Has the Messiah, or the messianic age, come? The answer lies in God's promise of a restored Israel.

Notes

[1] N. T. Wright, *Jesus and the Victory of God* (Minneapolis: Fortress Press, 1996) strongly insists that the "historically concrete worldview of the second-Temple period" would not have thought that the exile was over. "The point is that Jewish eschatology in the second-Temple period focused on the hope that that which had happened in the Babylonian exile, the triumph of paganism over Israel because of her sins, was still the dominant state of affairs, but would at last be undone" (xviii). Craig A. Evans, "Jesus and the Continuing Exile of Israel," *Jesus and the Restoration of Israel: A Critical Assessment of N. T. Wright's* Jesus and the Victory of God, ed. Carey C. Newman (Downers Grove, Ill.: InterVarsity Press, 1999), after reviewing the major texts, concludes: "Although one encounters differences in detail, a fairly consistent pattern emerges. Many Jews during the Second Temple period believed that the exile perdured. Most obviously, the exile was evident in the dispersion of the Jewish people and in the continuing foreign domination of Israel. Less obviously, the exile was evident in the failure on the part of many Jews to obey the law. Just exactly what was entailed in obedience to the law was itself a matter of dispute; and many groups and individuals were eager to make their views known" (90–1). Malachi's disillusionment with the abuses of his day (correctly referred to as 'post-exilic' insofar as he was writing after the return from Babylon in 538) could be an indicator of this view as well. By Jesus' day Judah had been ruled by successive foreign powers with the brief exception of the Hasmoneans (which carried its own problems of legitimacy) and had, of course, been ruled by the Romans since 63 B.C.E. In that sense, the exile was a continuing experience.

[2] J.P.M. Walsh, *The Mighty from Their Thrones: Power in the Biblical Tradition* (Philadelphia: Fortress Press, 1987) 147–8.

[3] Ibid., 147. Geza Vermes, *Jesus and the World of Judaism* (Philadelphia: Fortress Press, 1983) 32–5, outlines four views of the kingdom: (1) YHWH promises power and conquest as king of Israel (Pss 2:8-11; 99:1-3); (2) a royal Messiah will come (Ps Sol 17:23-32); (3) apocalyptic victory; (4) the nations will flock to Zion (Isa 60:1-6) with no violence or war. He sees Jesus as favoring the last.

[4] Walsh, *The Mighty from Their Thrones,* 148.

[5] For a good review of a wide variety of views, see William E. Arnal and Michel Desjardins, eds., *Whose Historical Jesus?* Studies in Christianity and Judaism 7 (Waterloo, Ontario: Wilfrid Laurier Press, 1997), especially the article on various views of apocalyptic by Edith M. Humphrey, "Will the Reader Understand? Apocalypse as Veil or Vision in Recent Historical-Jesus Studies" (ch. 18)

and the article on various views of Jesus' identity (a survey of full-length books between 1984–93) by Larry W. Hurtado, "A Taxonomy of Recent Historical-Jesus Work" (ch. 22). In a concluding article, "Making and Re-Making the Jesus-Sign: Contemporary Markings on the Body of Christ" (ch. 24), William E. Arnal asks: is the question whether Jesus was an "observant Jew" concerned with Torah, purity rules, Temple tax, etc. (as opposed to being a "Jewish Cynic"), or whether he had a mission to his people that demanded prophetic criticism of certain practices (308–13)? Arnal concludes that there is a point in common among the various authors: "Jesus is portrayed as re-active, and what he reacts to is the shifting economic and political organization of his culture, endeavoring to return to traditional patterns of social organization, or at least invoking them rhetorically in the face of, and as a foil to, configurations felt to be alienating" (318). Given the way the Gospels present Jesus as in conflict with the leadership, could he be viewed in any other way? In addition, as a minimum, I would be in sharp disagreement with those who deny to Jesus any interest in or concern for the social, economic, and political realities of his day, e.g., Vermes, *Jesus and the World of Judaism,* 50, where he speaks of "Jesus' total lack of interest in the economic and political realities of his age. He was not a social reformer or nationalistic revolutionary, notwithstanding recent claims to the contrary." See also J. Arthur Baird, *The Justice of God in the Teaching of Jesus* (London: SCM Press, 1963), who rightly states: "The thesis to be presented here is that the concept of justice is the heart of the prophetic concept of God, the central element in the gospel of Jesus, and the ultimate clue to his mission and message" (14), but then offers a treatment that is highly individualistic and overly spiritualized, verging on dualism, anti-Jewish, and negative about the human condition. Not surprisingly, he offers no significant analysis of the social reality in Jesus' day.

[6] William R. Herzog II, *Jesus, Justice, and the Reign of God: A Ministry of Liberation* (Louisville: Westminster John Knox Press, 2000) 70.

[7] Sean Freyne, *Galilee, Jesus and the Gospels* (Philadelphia: Fortress Press, 1988) 175: "What has emerged [as the conclusion to his chapter on 'The Social World of First-Century Galilee'] is a dominantly village and peasant ethos which forms a viable sub-culture in the heartland of Galilee, despite pressure from various quarters, most notably from the elites who formed the Herodian aristocracy within Antipas' territory, and the Jerusalem priestly ascendancy with both religious and secular claims on their allegiance." See also his article "Galilean Questions to Crossan's Mediterranean Jesus," ch. 6 in *Whose Historical Jesus?* ed. Arnal and Desjardins: "It is my opinion that a less rigid approach to the question of sources and a greater attention to the real social world of Galilee has a better chance of doing justice to the historical Jesus, however inaccessible that figure may still remain" (75).

[8] Bruce J. Malina, *The Social Gospel of Jesus: The Kingdom of God in Mediterranean Perspective* (Minneapolis: Fortress Press, 2001), maintains that in Jesus' day religion and economics were embedded in the belonging of kinship and the power of politics. "Hence, biblical documents reveal a vocabulary and syntax employed to realize a range of meanings expressing belonging (the dimension rooted in kinship) and power (the dimension rooted in politics), but almost nothing to express reasoned influence (the dimension rooted in the meaning of

religious institution) and inducement (the dimension rooted in economics)" (17). And so: "The scenario most befitting the story of Jesus is one of politically embedded religion. Jesus proclaims his message, describes his task, and directs his symbolic actions at the pillars of politically embedded Israelite Yahwism" (94). For a review of various approaches to the social sciences, see Carolyn Osiek, *What Are They Saying About the Social Setting of the New Testament?* rev. and expanded (Mahwah, N.J.: Paulist Press, 1992). Her second chapter (25–35) is a summary of Bruce Malina's earlier work, *The New Testament World: Insights from Cultural Anthropology* (Louisville: Westminster John Knox Press, 1993; Osiek refers to the earlier 1981 edition).

[9] E. P. Sanders, *Paul and Palestinian Judaism: A Comparison of Patterns of Religion* (Philadelphia: Fortress Press, 1977) characterizes this pattern as "covenantal nomism." At the conclusion to his study of Palestinian Judaism from 200 B.C.E. to 200 C.E., he states: "Because of the consistency with which covenantal nomism is maintained from early in the second century B.C.E. to late in the second century C.E., it must be hypothesized that covenantal nomism was *pervasive* in Palestine before 70. It was thus the basic *type* of religion known by Jesus and presumably by Paul" (426, emphasis in original).

[10] James H. Charlesworth and Loren L. Johns, eds., *Hillel and Jesus: Comparisons of Two Major Religious Leaders* (Minneapolis: Fortress Press, 1997), offer a variety of views on the relationship between the two. J. H. Charlesworth, "Hillel and Jesus: Why Comparisons Are Important" (3–30), considers them "the two most influential Jewish teachers in the period from Ezra to the destruction of 70" (4). And further: "This time of transition—from approximately 63 B.C.E., when Pompey entered the Land, to 132 C.E., when Bar Cosiba was defeated—produced *a standard script, text, collection or canon, and the first statutory prayers in Jewish liturgy*. . . . In the process all early Jewish groups—which totaled more than a dozen—were reduced to only two: one group followed the teachings of Hillel and the other the teachings of Jesus" (14, emphasis in original). He goes on to enumerate the major similarities and the major differences. On the other hand, A. Goshen Gottstein, "Hillel and Jesus: Are Comparisons Possible?" (31–55), emphasizes the contrasts.

[11] D. R. Schwartz, "Hillel and Scripture: From Authority to Exegesis," *Hillel and Jesus,* ed. Charlesworth and Johns, 335–62, sees Hillel as "a sage of the oral tradition" (337) rather than as an exegete of Scripture. The "replacement of argument from tradition by argument from exegesis is usually associated with the name of R. Akiba [+ ca. 135], who so developed exegesis that he became capable of reading virtually all traditions back into Scripture" (350). Hillel, on the other hand, "did not teach 'as one of the scribes'; he taught either directly out of Scripture, or on the basis of tradition, or, most characteristically, 'as one who had authority' [cf. Mark 1:22] . . . . In Jabneh, the main approach of rabbinic Judaism had become one which sought to anchor all divine law in Scripture. It would not be audacious to suggest that an important reason for the triumph of this textually bound approach in Judaism was the secession from Judaism of a religion whose founder, like Hillel, had preferred the other one" (360).

[12] Clemens Thoma, "Literary and Theological Aspects of the Rabbinic Parables," *Parable and Story in Judaism and Christianity,* ed. Clemens Thoma and

Michael Wyschogrod (Mahwah, N.J.: Paulist Press, 1989) 26–41, has a good analysis of the distinction between *mashal* (narrative level) and *nimshal* (normative level) in rabbinic parables (27–31) and affirms that "the rabbinic parables always have an ethical orientation" (38). Brad H. Young, *Jesus and His Jewish Parables: Rediscovering the Roots of Jesus' Teaching* (Mahwah, N.J.: Paulist Press, 1989), sees the distinction between parable *(mashal)* and explanation *(nimshal)* in rabbinic literature as also characteristic of Jesus whose purpose was to instruct (7, 37, 105, 221, 317–21). This volume, along with his *Jesus the Jewish Theologian* (Peabody, Mass.: Hendrickson, 1995), is valuable for the many references to rabbinic literature. Both of Young's volumes are heavily influenced by the work of David Flusser.

[13] On parables as stories that have metaphoric impact, see Michael L. Cook, "Jesus' Parables and the Faith That Does Justice," *Studies in the Spirituality of Jesuits* 24:5 (November 1992) 1–35; also, *Christology as Narrative Quest* (Collegeville: The Liturgical Press, 1997) 49–54. For an insightful analysis of parables as directed toward "unmasking the world of oppression" and "opening up new possibilities," see William R. Herzog II, *Parables as Subversive Speech: Jesus as Pedagogue of the Oppressed* (Louisville: Westminster John Knox Press, 1994).

[14] E. P. Sanders, *Jesus and Judaism* (Philadelphia: Fortress Press, 1985), observes: "The method which is being followed more and more, and the one which it seems necessary to follow in writing about Jesus, is to construct hypotheses which, on the one hand, do rest on material generally considered reliable without, on the other hand, being totally dependent on the authenticity of any given pericope" (3). Similar statements can be found in Ben F. Meyer, *The Aims of Jesus* (London: SCM Press, 1979); John Riches, *Jesus and the Transformation of Judaism* (New York: Seabury Press, 1982); Wright, *Jesus and the Victory of God;* and Herzog, *Jesus, Justice, and the Reign of God*. This chapter will not try to justify each and every claim as historically authentic, although such justification can usually be found in the authors cited in the notes. Whether one would dispute a particular historical claim or not, the important question is whether the hypothesis is sufficiently tested insofar as the data give a coherent and unified picture of the historical Jesus as a whole.

[15] Walsh, *The Mighty from Their Thrones*, 165–6, observes that the Hebrew root *nḥm* as at *naḥămû* (Isa 40:1, 2 times) can be translated into Greek as *metanoein* (repent) but also as *parakalein* (console). Thus, Jesus in the spirit of Isa 40:1 could also be saying: "Receive the consolation of YHWH."

[16] Richard J. Clifford, *Fair Spoken and Persuading: An Interpretation of Second Isaiah* (New York: Paulist Press, 1984). See ch. 2, n. 64.

[17] Employing his characteristic threefold repetition, Mark repeats *panta dunata* ("all things are possible") at 9:23 ("for one who believes"), at 10:27 ("for God"), and at 14:36 ("for you, Abba"). The third is the culmination of the three statements for Mark, but underlying all three is Jesus' call to rely completely upon YHWH.

[18] The traditional interpretation of this text has, of course, been quite otherwise, but contrary to those who think the Gospels were written as some sort of *apologia* to the Romans, Mark at least gives no indication of this, not even at the moment of Jesus' death and the centurion's so-called "confession" (15:39). The

centurion represents the satanic power of Rome that is crushing Jesus, and his words, while true, are ironic in that they represent the defeat of Rome. Earlier, it is always the demons and only the demons who know who Jesus is (1:24, 34; 3:11, 27; 5:7). The story of the demoniac on the other side of the sea (5:1-20), whose name is "legion" *(legiōn),* is clearly aimed at the Romans whose power has come to an end. For Mark, the way of the cross has rendered both Temple hegemony (15:38) and Roman power (15:39) ineffective. As a further confirmation, Peter's confession of Jesus as the Christ, while also true, is equally ironic. Peter is called Satan (8:33) because he cannot accept the cross. Finally, Luke (23:2) notes that one of the charges brought against Jesus was forbidding to give tribute to Caesar.

[19] Freyne, "Galilean Questions," 82. On Herod Antipas' cities and Jesus' avoidance of them, see Freyne, *Galilee, Jesus and the Gospels,* 136–43. For a recent book on Herod the Great and his family that gives good insight into the social situation of the times, see Peter Richardson, *Herod, King of the Jews and Friend of Romans* (Columbia: University of South Carolina Press, 1996).

[20] The independent parallel to Matt 17:20 at Luke 17:6 has a different metaphor, the notably deep-rooted sycamine (or mulberry) tree: "Be uprooted and planted in the sea." Mark 11:23 (= Matt 21:21) mixes the image by having the mountain taken up and cast into the sea. He places the saying in the context of the Temple incident and the withering of the fig tree, thereby signaling that the Temple no longer has validity. This is Mark's view, not Jesus', but the association with the Temple may well go back to Jesus.

[21] E. P. Sanders, *Jewish Law from Jesus to the Mishnah* (London: SCM Press & Philadelphia: Trinity Press International, 1990) 90. This is the conclusion to his chapter on "The Synoptic Jesus and the Law." He reviews the disputes about sabbath, purity, food, etc., to show that, whether historically authentic or not, they all fall within the acceptable range of disagreement in first-century disputes about the law.

[22] Marcus J. Borg, *Jesus, a New Vision: Spirit, Culture, and the Life of Discipleship* (San Francisco: HarperCollins, 1987) 16. It is the great virtue of this book to bring together the understanding of charismatics as "people who know the world of Spirit firsthand" (27) so that "the heart of the biblical tradition is 'charismatic,' its origin lying in the experience of Spirit-endowed people" (32), and Jesus as such a man of Spirit who "sought to transform his social world by creating an alternative community structured around compassion" (142). N. T. Wright in his otherwise excellent *Jesus and the Victory of God* does not develop the theme of the Spirit as of central importance in Jesus' life and mission.

[23] Vermes, *Jesus and the World of Judaism,* 11ff., suggests four reasons why Jesus gave offense to Pharisees and others: (1) lack of expertise, especially in *halakhah* (see John 7:15: "How does this man have such learning [literally, 'know his letters'], when he has never been taught [*mē memathēkōs,* literally, 'not having sat as a disciple' at the feet of a teacher, i.e., rabbi"]); (2) tolerance of those who neglect certain traditional (not biblical) customs (e.g., the practice of fasting other than on the Day of Atonement at Mark 2:18-22); (3) table-fellowship with publicans and whores; (4) the claim to authority that comes from the Spirit. In my view, the last would seem to be the most serious since it gives credence to all the other claims and activities. Luke 4:16-20 presents Jesus as facing this

challenge at the very beginning of his mission. Mark 11:27-33 places it in the context of the Temple incident but has Jesus refer back to the baptism of John when he received the Spirit.

[24] John J. Pilch, *Healing in the New Testament: Insights from Medical and Mediterranean Anthropology* (Minneapolis: Fortress Press, 2000) 141.

[25] African culture today would have a better understanding of Jesus' practice of healing. See Grant LeMarquand, "The Historical Jesus and African New Testament Scholarship," ch. 13 in *Whose Historical Jesus?* ed. Arnal and Desjardins. He refers to an article by E. A. Obeng, "The Significance of the Miracles of Resuscitation and Its Implication for the Church in Africa," *Bible Bhashyam* 18 (1992): "Obeng proceeds to show that the denial of the existence of spiritual forces by the mission-founded churches has created a kind of religious schizophrenia among African Christians, who go to church for salvation from sin, but return to traditional religious practices to deal with sickness, evil spirits or troublesome ancestors" (175).

[26] Pilch, *Healing in the New Testament,* 51.

[27] Malina, *The Social Gospel of Jesus,* 100: "But in a moral context, rich meant powerful due to greed, avarice, and exploitation, while poor meant weak due to inability to maintain one's inherited social station." He comments that the issue is not whether one is rich or poor in a limited goods society but how one can maintain one's inherited status in an honorable way.

[28] Pilch, *Healing in the New Testament,* 121.

[29] Herzog, *Jesus, Justice, and the Reign of God,* 124–32. Sanders, *Jewish Law,* 62, disagrees with this interpretation: "Thus, though Jesus' pronouncement might conceivably have been seen as challenging the priestly prerogative, there is no evidence that anyone understood it to do so, nor that the priests thought that only they could discuss God's forgiveness." One of the main theses of Herzog's book is that Jesus sought to separate the Temple from the land in order to renew the covenant in village life, as opposed to the domination systems of Temple and kingship. See ch. 9, "Temple, the Land, and the Reign of God" (191–216): "This chapter proposes that Jesus' strategy was to separate the temple from the land and to critique the domination systems found throughout his world" (191). There is truth in this, but I would side more with the view that Jesus did not oppose the Temple as such nor its legitimate practice of sacrifices but only the abuses stemming from the wealthy aristocrats associated with the Temple.

[30] Herzog, *Jesus, Justice, and the Reign of God,* 152–4, following Jacob Neusner's view, comments: "The Pharisees were a table companionship sect that attempted to transform every meal into a ritual of purity equal to that of the priests consuming a meal in the temple" (153). He sees Jesus' practice as challenging or contradicting Pharisaic practice. Sanders, *Jewish Law,* in his third chapter, "Did the Pharisees Eat Ordinary Food in Purity?" disagrees with the almost unanimous scholarly opinion, including that of Neusner, "that the Pharisees ate ordinary food at their own tables as if they were priests in the temple" (131). He sees the Pharisees as primarily concerned about a careful study of the law, and of their own extra-biblical tradition, as well as about life after death. They also sought a special degree of purity for themselves but did not impose an impossible legalism on the average person. They were, however, concerned to protect the priest-

hood and the Temple from impurity (236). As to the charge of Pharisaic exclusivism, he distinguishes between a "party" that maintains a sense of self-identity and a "sect" that cuts itself off from society: "The distinction between sect and party seems to me perfectly adequate: the Pharisees and Sadducees were parties; the group of CD *[Covenant of Damascus]* were a party, though more extremist than the Pharisees (CD accepts the temple and the sacrifices); the Qumran community was a sect" (241).

[31] Borg, *Jesus, a New Vision,* 142, although he treats the parables in a peripheral way rather than seeing them as central to Jesus' message about the kingdom.

[32] Herzog, *Jesus, Justice, and the Reign of God,* 199, summarizing his interpretation of Mark 4:3-9 and 4:26-29, concludes: "In telling these parables, Jesus was driving a wedge between the temple and the land." He sees the contrast between the predators ("birds devoured," "sun scorched," and "thorns choked") and the good land that produces abundance in the parable of the sower to be raising the question why the peasants live in poverty if the land is so abundantly productive (which the Temple is supposed to guarantee). The problem is not with the land but with the distribution of what is produced. "To blame the scarcity on their inability to fulfill the Torah [purity codes, tithes] is to distract the peasants from the true source of their poverty, the ruling elites who take almost everything and leave almost nothing" (195). In the other parable, the focus is on the land which produces "of itself" (4:28: *automatē*), not as dependent on the Temple system.

[33] Herzog, *Parables as Subversive Speech,* treats these parables in Part 3, "Opening Up New Possibilities: Challenging the Limits."

[34] Ibid., 232. For an excellent analysis of the parable and various scholarly opinions about it, see the whole of ch. 12, "Justice at the Gate?" 215–32. The summary in the text is based on Herzog's analysis.

[35] Ibid., 192. Again, the summary in the text is dependent upon the whole of ch. 10, "The Deviant and Prominent Toll Collectors," 173–93.

[36] Joachim Jeremias, *New Testament Theology: The Proclamation of Jesus* (New York: Scribner's, 1971) 111–2, proposes F. W. Danker's suggestion as a plausible interpretation of Matt 11:12; namely, that the kingdom of heaven has experienced real conflict during Jesus' ministry but that those whom his opponents contemn as "violent intruders" *(biastai)* are the ones who are truly "grasping it" *(harpazousin autēn).* A similar idea, specifying "the toll collectors and the prostitutes," can be found at Matt 21:31b-32 (cf. Luke 7:29-30). Young, *Jesus the Jewish Theologian,* 51–5, interprets the text in the light of Mic 2:13: "The one who breaks out *[haporēṣ]* will go up before them; they will break through *[pārṣû]* and pass the gate, going out by it. Their king will pass on before them, the LORD at their head." The image is of sheep breaking out of a makeshift enclosure, so that Matt 11:12 is saying: "the kingdom of heaven is breaking forth *[biazetai]*, and those breaking forth *[biastai]* are pursuing (or seeking) it *[harpazousin autēn]*." In either case, the image is of those who have been oppressed or contained and are now experiencing a new and exciting freedom.

[37] Ben F. Meyer, *Christus Faber: The Master-Builder and the House of God* (Allison Park, Pa.: Pickwick Publications, 1992) 1: "*Christus Faber*/'Christ the Artisan' alludes to a classic messianic image, the Messiah as master-builder of the house of God. This was among the most traditional and comprehensive ways in which

Jesus described his mission. The mission was the eschatological ('end-time oriented') restoration of God's people." Associated images would include king, shepherd, architect, etc. This does not mean that Jesus specifically identified himself as Messiah, something that would be open to misunderstanding (as at Mark 8:27-33 par.), but that the five "commonly accepted" data (59)—proclamation of the reign "at hand"; authority; works of healing and exorcism; the action in the Temple; and crucifixion as "the king of the Jews"—have a cumulative effect: "Jesus' [unique] consciousness of being the bearer of a divinely appointed, climactic and definitive, mission to Israel" (67). Although emphasizing newness (new covenant, new sanctuary, new cult), Meyer connects Jesus' mission to the fulfillment of Scripture according to God's *ṣĕdāqâ* and *ʾĕmûnâ*.

[38] John P. Meier, "Are There Historical Links between the Historical Jesus and the Christian Ministry?" *Theology Digest* 47 (Winter 2000) 311: "For all the structural elements Jesus created, his itinerant ministry of two years and some months was of necessity fluid and shifting." This Bellarmine Lecture draws on his forthcoming book: *A Marginal Jew: Rethinking the Historical Jesus,* vol. 3: *Companions and Competitors* (New York: Doubleday, 2001).

[39] Ibid., 305: "[Some present-day questers for the historical Jesus] champion a thesis, cherished by many within the Jesus Seminar, that Jesus was a structureless, radical egalitarian. He was against all structures, groups, or authorities that mediated God's presence and power to human beings. Or, as John Dominic Crossan likes to put it, Jesus was against all the client-patronage systems and the systems of brokerage of power on which the ancient world ran—and, dare we say, on which much of our modern world runs as well." He refers to John Dominic Crossan, *The Historical Jesus: The Life of a Mediterranean Jewish Peasant* (San Francisco: HarperCollins, 1991).

[40] Ibid., 307. See the similar statement cited in ch. 1 by Anthony J. Saldarini, *Matthew's Christian-Jewish Community* (Chicago: University of Chicago Press, 1994) 39.

[41] Sanders, *Paul and Palestinian Judaism,* in discussing the nature of Tannaitic literature, gives a good description of *halakhah:* "to determine whether or not a biblical passage does in fact constitute a commandment, if there can be any doubt; to establish the application of a biblical commandment; to define its precise scope and meaning; and to determine precisely what must be done in order to fulfill it" (76). He comments further: "Whether lenient or strict, the Rabbinic definitions of what the biblical law requires, as well as Rabbinic enactments, were always capable of being performed. The legal rulings do not hold up an ideal which is impossible of achievement" (80).

[42] Robert Banks, *Jesus and the Law in the Synoptic Tradition* (Cambridge: Cambridge University Press, 1975) 172, in discussing Jesus' attitude toward the law, rejects categories like exposition, completion, radicalization, sharpening, and abrogation. Of the three remaining alternatives, he also rejects new legislation replacing the old and will accept fulfillment only in relation to Jesus' mission, i.e., his teaching and practice culminating in the cross, so that Jesus completely *transforms* the law: "It is *to* that ministry that the Law 'prophetically' pointed, and it is only in so far as it has been taken up *into* that teaching and completely transformed that it lives on" (242, emphasis in original). Sanders, *Jesus and Judaism,*

247, refers to this section of Banks and comments: "Banks proposes that Jesus took up no attitude towards the law, but simply bypassed ('surpassed') it. He regards Jesus as having adopted a position which was not in conscious relation to the law one way or another, although opposition to the law was latent in his position." Sanders agrees that Jesus was not a "midrashist," i.e., an exegetical commentator on Torah, but questions whether Jesus would not have known that to question or oppose part of the law is to question or oppose the whole since the law is unitary. Sanders' own question is whether Jesus challenged the adequacy of the Mosaic dispensation as such (250).

43 For a resolute attempt to understand all six antitheses as being in conformity with the authority of the Torah in the Hebrew Scriptures, see Roland H. Worth Jr., *The Sermon on the Mount: Its Old Testament Roots* (Mahwah, N.J.: Paulist Press, 1997). Banks, *Jesus and the Law,* 182–235, sees all six antitheses as "surpassing" or "transcending" the law. He concludes his discussion of Matt 5:17-20 (203–26) by affirming that the issue for Matthew is not Jesus' stance toward the law but how the law stands with regard to him, his person, teaching, and conduct. Sanders, *Jesus and Judaism,* 260–4, doubts the authenticity of Matt 5:17–6:18, except for the prayer (6:9-13) and the saying on divorce in some form, because Jesus is presented as calling his followers to be more righteous than the Pharisees *by the same standard.* In any event, he does not think the antitheses would tell us anything more than what we already know; namely, "that Jesus did not oppose the Mosaic law, but held it in some ways to be neither adequate nor final" (263). For a good review of diverse scholarly opinions on the whole Sermon on the Mount, see Warren Carter, *What Are They Saying About Matthew's Sermon on the Mount?* (Mahwah, N.J.: Paulist Press, 1994).

44 Banks, *Jesus and the Law,* 156–7, follows the linguistic analysis of Bruce Vawter and reads the exceptive clause at Matt 5:32 and 19:9 as a typical Matthean precision that rejects the permission in Deut 24:1 and so should be translated: "the permission of Deut 24:1 notwithstanding."

45 Banks sees Matt 5:32 as more in line with the Jewish understanding of adultery as a sin against the man; i.e., the divorce is located "not in the further marriage of the divorcing partner [the man], but in the further marriage of the divorced wife" (ibid., 192).

46 Matthew is the only evangelist who uses the term *praüs* and it is clear that Jesus is the embodiment of its meaning. At 11:29, Jesus says: "Learn from me, for I am humbly obedient *[praüs eimi kai tapeinos]* in heart" (author's trans.). That "humbly obedient" is preferable to the usual "meek" or "gentle" seems to be clinched by the third use at 21:5, citing Zech 9:9, where Jesus is the "humbly obedient" *(praüs)* king coming to Zion in fulfillment of God's will. For Matthew, Jesus not only proclaims God's will, and especially his righteousness, but he does it. Thus, in Matthew's view, there is a natural connection of the third beatitude to the fourth on righteousness, not to mention to the two preceding beatitudes on the poor and the suffering. This is Matthew's construction, but the themes cohere with Jesus' historical mission.

47 The reconstruction of the original prayer by Jeremias, *New Testament Theology,* 193–203, follows the length of Luke 11:2-4 but uses the aorist rather than the present tense of Matt 6:11 ("give us today!") and the perfect tense rather than the

present at Matt 6:12 ("as we have forgiven," understood as a *perfectum coincidentiae,* i.e., the divine forgiveness is effective insofar as we forgive one another's debts). However, I would agree with Young, *Jesus and His Jewish Parables,* 31–3, who prefers to translate *ton arton hēmōn ton epiousion* not as "tomorrow's bread today" in a more strictly eschatological sense, but as "our necessary bread" in a more immediate sense of the reality of today. He sees *epi ousia* as underlying *epiousion* with the meaning of "necessary for existence."

[48] Herzog, *Jesus, Justice, and the Reign of God,* 155–67.

[49] Ibid., 166. The distinction between purity codes and debt codes is found in Fernando Belo, *A Materialist Reading of the Gospel of Mark,* trans. Matthew J. O'Connell (Maryknoll, N.Y.: Orbis Books, 1981) 37–59.

[50] Martin Hengel, *The Charismatic Leader and His Followers,* trans. James Greig (New York: Crossroad, 1981) 14. This refers to the Greco-Roman world as well as to Judaism.

[51] Sanders, *Jesus and Judaism,* 252.

[52] Ibid., 254 (emphasis in original). He is disagreeing with the view of Banks, *Jesus and the Law,* 96–8, who sees it as "a purely proverbial" saying with "no actual referent(s) in view" to emphasize "the priority of discipleship over domestic responsibilities." Sanders gives a "modest conclusion": "At least once Jesus was willing to say that following him superseded the requirements of piety and Torah. This may show that Jesus was prepared, if necessary, to challenge the adequacy of the Mosaic dispensation" (255). Thus, for Banks the saying is "incidental" in relation to either the oral or the written law and indeed bypasses it, whereas for Sanders it is exceptional: "Should this be generalized, or should we take it to be a rare, perhaps unrepeated instance in which Jesus put the call to follow him above even the law?" (254).

[53] Sanders, *Jesus and Judaism,* 133: "I regard most of the exegetical efforts of the last decades as proving a negative: analysis of the sayings material does not succeed in giving us a picture of Jesus which is convincing and which answers historically important questions."

[54] Meier, "Are There Historical Links?" 308–10, to which the summary in the text is indebted. He goes on to enumerate other distinctive identity markers, such as the practice of baptism, a joyous table-fellowship with toll-collectors and sinners that precludes fasting, a special disciples' prayer, and as we will treat later one last "supper of salvation."

[55] On the authenticity and meaning of the saying, see Sanders, *Jesus and Judaism,* 98–106, and Marius Reiser, *Jesus and Judgment: The Eschatological Proclamation in Its Jewish Context,* trans. Linda M. Maloney (Minneapolis: Fortress Press, 1997) 258–62.

[56] Norbert Lohfink, *Option for the Poor: The Basic Principle of Liberation Theology in the Light of the Bible,* trans. Linda M. Maloney (N. Richland Hills, Tex.: BIBAL Press, 1987, 1995) 63. He interprets Matt 25:31-46, "the least of these," as referring to "the poor of Yahweh" now understood as Jesus' brothers and sisters, i.e., new community (NRSV translates v. 40 as "one of the least of these who are members of my family"). If the Israelites are judged by how they treat the poor, by how they respond to Jesus' vision of the community, the nations will be judged by how they treat this new community which consists of "the poor of Yahweh."

[57] Ben F. Meyer, "Jesus and the Remnant of Israel," *Journal of Biblical Literature* LXXXIV (1965) 123–30, proposes a "revised state of the question" on two points: "first, the question of the remnant is situated in its rightful context, that of judgment, and specifically that of the gospel data bearing on Jesus and judgment; the second point is clarification of how the intent to save the remnant of Israel can coexist with a universalist salvific mission" (129).

[58] Sanders, *Jesus and Judaism,* 207.

[59] David Flusser, "Jesus, His Ancestry, and the Commandment of Love," *Jesus' Jewishness,* ed. James H. Charlesworth (New York: Crossroad, 1991) 165.

[60] J.D.G. Dunn, "Jesus and Factionalism in Early Judaism: How Serious Was the Factionalism of Late Second Temple Judaism?" *Hillel and Jesus,* ed. Charlesworth and Johns, 156–75, sees the contrast between righteous (pious, *ḥasid*) and sinner (impious, lawless) as much more divisive: "In short, the seriousness of designating a fellow Jew 'sinner' was tantamount to *denying that person's status within the covenant and thus as a recipient of God's saving righteousness*" (164, emphasis in original). And further, *"to designate another as 'sinner' in early Jewish tradition was to name that person as one who as such was disowned by God, and who, in status as a sinner, was liable to the fearful judgments illustrated above"* (170, emphasis in original). Thus, "sinners" were outside the covenant and excluded from salvation. The distinctive stand of Jesus at Mark 2:17 is seen in the unqualified character of his invitation to sinners that implies a criticism of the attitude of the righteous toward sinners. Dunn draws the further conclusion that Jesus was protesting such factionalism precisely because covenant status was being denied to some Jews.

[61] Reiser, *Jesus and Judgment,* 302. In summarizing the sources, he has found sayings from Q, Mark, Matthew, and Luke; in other words, not just from Q but throughout the synoptic tradition: "more than a quarter of the traditional discourse material of Jesus is concerned with the theme of the final judgment" (304).

[62] Meyer, "Jesus and the Remnant," 128, sets Jesus' mission in the historical context of John the Baptist's theology of the "open remnant," i.e., not limited to a given group but "defined by the recognition that a summons addressed to *all* may well be answered only by *some*" (emphasis in original). Chapter 5 of *Christus Faber* is entitled: "Many (= All) Are Called, but Few (= Not All) Are Chosen" (81–90, referring to Matt 22:14). This, of course, is in line with the "apocalyptic eschatology" of Isaiah 65–66 (especially 65:1-16) which Marius Reiser frequently cites as background to John the Baptist and Jesus. Reiser, *Jesus and Judgment,* 29: "the 'servants' of YHWH, who will also constitute the community of the end time, are here called 'the chosen' for the first time . . . in 65:9, 15, 22. This designation will be taken up later, especially by eschatologically oriented groups and the communities that preserved apocalyptic traditions. But with this the idea of election is transferred from Israel as a whole to one or several groups within the people, an event whose significance for the history of this people and the ecclesiological self-interpretation of such groups and circles, for example, the Essenes of Qumran, can scarcely be overestimated. This development may have found its first literary expression in Trito-Isaiah."

[63] Reiser, *Jesus and Judgment,* 315.

[64] Ibid., 254.

[65] Ibid., 311.

[66] For exposition and analysis of these sayings, see Kim Huat Tan, *The Zion Traditions and the Aims of Jesus* (Cambridge: Cambridge University Press, 1997), Part II, "The Sayings," chs. 3, 4, 5. I am taking the references in the first person at Luke 13:34-35 par. as referring to YHWH rather than to Jesus.

[67] Ibid., Part III, "The Actions," chs. 6, 7, 8.

[68] Sanders, *Jesus and Judaism,* 307: "The question of Jesus' self-claim has, to understate the case, vexed scholars—it seems to me unduly. Jesus taught about the *kingdom;* he was executed as would-be *king;* and his disciples, after his death, expected him to return to establish the *kingdom.* These points are indisputable. Almost equally indisputable is the fact that the disciples thought that they would have some role in the kingdom. We should, I think, accept the obvious: Jesus taught his disciples that he himself would play the principal role in the kingdom" (emphasis in original). Tan, *The Zion Traditions,* 156: Jesus challenges Jerusalem "to recognize in him the divinely appointed agent of restoration (Q 13.34-5) and in this particular hour, the time of restoration."

[69] Donahue, *What Does the Lord Require?* 31–2, gives a helpful summary of terminology for the poor and the powerless in the biblical tradition. For an excellent analysis of the beatitude for the poor in Luke (6:20) and its linguistic background, see L. John Topel, *Children of a Compassionate God: A Theological Exegesis of Luke 6:20-49* (Collegeville: The Liturgical Press, 2001) 55–96.

[70] Tan, *The Zion Traditions,* 181. Sanders, *Jesus and Judaism,* after analyzing various scholarly views which he rejects, especially purification, symbolic inclusion of Gentiles, and protest against Temple officers and the Sadducean party, and after considering the sayings about the destruction of the Temple, sums up his position: "Thus we conclude that Jesus publicly predicted or threatened the destruction of the temple, that the statement was shaped by his expectation of the arrival of the eschaton, that he probably also expected a new temple to be given by God from heaven, and that he made a demonstration which prophetically symbolized the coming event" (75). Herzog, *Jesus, Justice, and the Reign of God,* is close to Tan in seeing the Temple action as an attack on oppressive economic practices: "The temple was, therefore, at the very heart of the system of economic exploitation made possible by monetizing the economy and the concentration of wealth made possible by investing the temple and its leaders with the powers and rewards of a collaborating aristocracy. . . . The temple was not only a religious and political institution; it was a major economic force, controlling massive amounts of money while continuing to accumulate more. All of the functionaries mentioned in the incident in the temple were part of this system and served it" (137). However, he is closer to Sanders in seeing Jesus' action as symbolizing the destruction of the Temple because it had become an "oppressive institution" (143).

[71] For our purposes, it is not necessary to specify the exact time and place of Jesus' last meal with the Twelve, if it can be done at all. The Synoptics portray it as the Passover meal. John 13:1 places it before the feast of Passover. Paul simply says, "on the night when he was betrayed" (1 Cor 11:23). What is important is the association with Passover, Zion, and betrayal. John P. Meier, "The Eucharist at the Last Supper: Did It Happen?" *Theology Digest* 42 (1995) 335–51, argues not

that the Last Supper was a Eucharist but that it was in essence a historical event. He argues that the earliest available tradition includes the supper, the betrayal, the key actions (taking, blessing, breaking, giving), and the two sayings (as he reconstructs them): "This is my flesh" and "This cup is the covenant in my blood." Many scholars have argued that the independent logion at Mark 14:25 is historical, without accepting the fuller tradition that Meier argues for.

[72] The betrayal by one of the Twelve is certainly a historical datum on the basis of embarrassment alone. Sanders, citing Schweitzer, proposes: "*what* Judas betrayed (a point on which the Gospels are unhelpful) was that Jesus and his small band thought of him as 'king'" (*Jesus and Judaism,* 309, emphasis in original). I doubt that Jesus thought of himself as "king" (cf. John 6:15) in a way that would have been threatening to either Temple authorities or Romans, but I have no doubt that it was the most effective charge brought against him as the titulus on the cross attests.

[73] Raymond E. Brown, *The Gospel According to John (I–XII)* (New York: Doubleday, 1966) 284.

[74] Luke omits Mark 10:45 (= Matt 20:28) with its reference to the Suffering Servant ("to give his life as a ransom for many") and substitutes a saying about being among the disciples "as one who serves" (Luke 22:27). It seems unlikely that he would have omitted it once and then emphasized it with a double reference in 22:19b-20. In addition, 22:16, 18 (with a cup saying already at v. 17) emphasize the words of Mark 14:25 as Luke's interpretive key to Jesus' intention.

[75] On the historicity of Mark 9:31a; 14:21, 25, 41, see Michael L. Cook, *The Jesus of Faith* (Mahwah, N.J.: Paulist Press, 1981) 64–6.

[76] Tan, *The Zion Traditions,* 219.

[77] Meier, "The Eucharist at the Last Supper," 349–50.

[78] Walsh, *The Mighty from Their Thrones,* 170. This is the last sentence of his book.

Conclusion

"All the Words That the Lord Has Spoken We Will Do" (Exod 24:3)

This book has not addressed the eventual triumph of both Rabbinic Judaism and Gentile Christianity and the corresponding failure of a more Jewish Christianity.[1] It has centered rather on our common root, the Hebrew Bible, and the relationship of the Jewish prophet Jesus of Nazareth to his ancestral heritage. The correspondence between the biblical notion of justice and Jesus' proclamation of the reign of God raises, it seems to me, a number of questions for both Jews and Christians. As such, it also provides a common ground or lens for Jewish-Christian dialogue. It is the hope of this book that the focus upon justice in the biblical sense may lead to a deepening of that dialogue. In view of the history of Christian persecution of the Jews, culminating in the demonic horror of the Shoah (Holocaust), and the subsequent establishment of the State of Israel, with its concurrent struggle over Palestinian rights to land and home, we conclude with questions for both Jews and Christians.[2] The intent here as throughout the book is not to ignore the real and clear differences between Judaism and Christianity as distinct religions and so to absorb or reduce one into the other, but to emphasize patterns of concern that are parallel in each.[3]

Can Jews and Christians agree that it is more important to be doers of God's will than mere hearers (Exod 24:3; Mark 3:35 par.; Matt 7:21; Jas 2:14-26)?[4] While historically it was not possible for Jewish Christians to maintain their Jewish identity,[5] is it possible for Christians today to be Christians without recognizing the Jewish origins of Christianity in Jesus and his first followers? Can Christians recognize that, while only Israel has Israel's relationship to God, they too hear the story of Israel through the story of Jesus as both their own and yet different?[6] Can Jews hear the proclamation of Jesus in his historical mission as corresponding to the deepest intentions of covenantal loyalty and fidelity?

Can both Jews and Christians recognize that the covenant cannot be maintained without justice?[7] Does YHWH still look for justice and see bloodshed, for righteousness and hear a cry (Isa 5:7)? Can either Jews or Christians claim the exclusive status of victim if they have victims of their own?[8] Can Jews and Christians recognize together that "without Israel and its Torah there is no universal salvation from the hand of God,"[9] that "salvation is from the Jews" (John 4:22)? Can we both recognize that, as Jesus stood at the Temple gate and looked for the return of YHWH to Zion, we are all called to build the Temple in our own day through study and prayer and to make the world "messiah worthy"?[10] Does this not mean that every exercise of authority and power must be in service to the most vulnerable, to the widow, the orphan, the stranger, so that no longer is there anyone poor and oppressed among us?

If, as we have been suggesting, the mission of Jesus expressed in his words and deeds and his personal relationship to the God of Israel is inseparable from the *tôrâ* of Moses, should we not examine more closely our common need for YHWH's *mišpaṭ* and how it is to be realized in practice today?[11] Does not the Jewish ideal of *tikkun olam* (repairing the world, restoring creation to its original perfection) resonate with the Christian hope for the full and final arrival of God's reign? Are we not called to work together to build the earth so that God will dwell among us again? Is not God's dwelling place in Jerusalem so that restoring the world cannot be separated from the restoration of Israel? Does not the fate of Torah depend on the fate of the Suffering Servant? Do we not share a pattern of chosenness, mission, and suffering because God chooses carefully and well those who will fulfill his *ṣĕdāqâ*?[12]

Finally, are we rivals for our father's unique blessing, as Jon Levenson says, or are we twin sons with different missions to preserve the family heritage, as Alan Segal maintains? Has God only one blessing?[13] Is not the blessing of Jacob-Israel, a blessing Jesus also proclaimed, the hope of the nations? "Justice, and only justice, you shall pursue, so that you may live and occupy the land that the LORD your God is giving you" (Deut 16:20).

Notes

[1] Philip S. Alexander, "'The Parting of the Ways' from the Perspective of Rabbinic Judaism," *Jews and Christians: The Parting of the Ways. A.D. 70 to 135*, ed. James D. G. Dunn (Grand Rapids, Mich.: Eerdmans Publishing, 1999) 1–25, concludes: "Jewish Christianity was finally destroyed between the upper and nether millstone of triumphant Gentile Christianity and triumphant Rabbinism" (24). Alan F. Segal, *Rebecca's Children: Judaism and Christianity in the Roman World* (Cambridge, Mass.: Harvard University Press, 1986) 160–2, discusses "the dynamics of separation" in which the biggest casualty was Jewish Christianity. For an interesting attempt to establish the earliest community's self-understanding based on the first chapters of Acts, see Ben F. Meyer, "The Initial Self-Understanding of the Church," *Catholic Biblical Quarterly* XXVII (January 1965) 35–42. He proposes five categories from the Hebrew Scriptures that indicate it understood itself as "the community of the last days": the community of the outpoured Spirit, eschatological Zion, the remnant of the last days, the heritage of Abraham, and the new *qahal*. On the crucial shift from the *hebraioi* of Jerusalem to the *hellenistai* in Acts, see Ben F. Meyer, *The Early Christians: Their World Mission and Self-Discovery* (Wilmington, Del.: Michael Glazier, 1986) 53–83.

[2] The same questions could be addressed to Muslims, but one would need to include a study of the *Qur'ān.*

[3] The book edited by Tikva Frymer-Kensky and others, *Christianity in Jewish Terms* (Boulder, Colo.: Westview Press, 2000), takes this approach around a variety of themes.

[4] I emphasize the Christian texts because it is often said that, while Jews are more concerned about practice *(halakhah)*, Christians are more concerned about belief (doctrines). This is a false dichotomy. Patrick J. Hartin, *A Spirituality of Perfection: Faith in Action in the Letter of James* (Collegeville: The Liturgical Press, 1999), comments: "The Letter of James holds more in common with Judaism than in separation from it. James offers a unique possibility to forge a dialogue between Judaism and Christianity" (165). He sees the notion of perfection as corresponding to Jewish traditions of wholeness (corresponding to the original idea of creation), wholehearted dedication to the Lord, and obedience to the Law in both James (89–92) and Matthew (133–8).

[5] Michael Wyschogrod, "A Jewish Reading of St. Thomas Aquinas on the Old Law," *Understanding Scripture: Explorations of Jewish and Christian Traditions of Interpretation*, ed. Clemens Thoma and Michael Wyschogrod (Mahwah, N.J.: Paulist Press, 1987) 125–38, makes the interesting observation: "That the difference between Jew and Gentile might in some sense remain real after Christ never occurs to Thomas. To be more specific, he does not entertain the possibility that Jewish Christians ought to maintain a Jewish identity in the Church by continuing to live under the Mosaic Law, while sharing with Gentile Christians their faith in Christ" (137).

[6] Paul M. Van Buren, "Acts 2:1-13—The Truth of an Unlikely Tale," *The Return to Scripture in Judaism and Christianity: Essays in Postcritical Scriptural Interpretation*, ed. Peter Ochs (Mahwah, N.J.: Paulist Press, 1993) 295–307, develops this theme: "The church is a linguistic community in the special sense that it is

a community other than Israel that hears Israel's story by way of the story of Jesus as also its own" (301).

[7] Abraham J. Heschel, *The Prophets,* vol. I (Peabody, Mass.: Prince Press, 1962; HarperCollins, 1969) 210 (see Chapter 2 above).

[8] For a perspective on victims, see Andrew Sung Park and Susan L. Nelson, eds., *The Other Side of Sin: Woundedness from the Perspective of the Sinned-Against* (Albany: State University of New York Press, 2001). Also, on mimetic violence, Rene Girard, *I See Satan Fall Like Lightning,* trans. James G. Williams (Maryknoll, N.Y.: Orbis Books, 2001; orig. in French, 1999) and, for a biblical perspective on Girard's theory, James G. Williams, *The Bible, Violence, and the Sacred: Liberation from the Myth of Sanctioned Violence* (Valley Forge, Pa.: Trinity Press International, 1991).

[9] Norbert Lohfink and Erich Zenger, *The God of Israel and the Nations: Studies in Isaiah and the Psalms,* trans. Everett R. Kalin (Collegeville: The Liturgical Press, 2000) 192. This again is the main theme of their book.

[10] Elliott R. Wolfson, "Judaism and Incarnation: The Imaginal Body of God," *Christianity in Jewish Terms,* ed. Frymer-Kensky and others, 239–54, emphasizes "the imaginal body of God, a symbolic construct that allows human consciousness to access the transcendent reality as a concrete form manifest primarily (if not exclusively) in the sacred space of the two major forms of worship of the heart: prayer and study" (240). Menachem Kellner, "How Ought a Jew View Christian Beliefs About Redemption?" *Christianity in Jewish Terms,* ed. Frymer-Kensky and others, 269–75, concludes (in disagreement with Paul): "The question that Jews must ask is: What must we do in order to make the world messiah-worthy?" (275).

[11] David Novak, "Mitsvah," *Christianity in Jewish Terms,* ed. Frymer-Kensky and others, 115–26, makes this point: "The great divide between Judaism and Christianity does not revolve around whether law is or is not part of the relationship with God. Instead, it is better to say that the need for law, which is the keeping of the commandments of the Lord God of Israel, is what is common to both Judaism and Christianity. How could the Lord God of Israel, the creator of heaven and earth, whom both Jews and Christians worship, not command us? Is not every act in relation to this God a response to one kind of commandment or another? Is not our relationship with this God a covenant? And is not a covenant a political reality? And could there be any polity not governed by law? So, *the* divide between us is not over law per se. The divide is over *what* those immutable commandments are, and this *what* depends on *when* and *where* one hears them and how one is to do them" (117, emphasis in original).

[12] Leora Batnitzky, "On the Suffering of God's Chosen: Christian Views in Jewish Terms," *Christianity in Jewish Terms,* ed. Frymer-Kensky and others, 203–20, says: "For both traditions, suffering, chosenness, and a theological and moral mission to the nations of the world are intimately connected; therefore, suffering is not an isolated issue that can be separated from the meaning of each faith community. Each community finds this meaning by interpreting its historical reality through the lens of a scriptural tradition" (206). I would disagree with her view, however, that Christians consider suffering necessary and inevitable because of fallen human nature and so "intrinsically valuable" (213). See in this

connection John C. Cavadini, "The Meaning and Value of Suffering: A Christian Response to Leora Batnitzky," *Christianity in Jewish Terms,* ed. Frymer-Kensky and others, 229–37.

[13] Jon Levenson, *The Death and Resurrection of the Beloved Son: The Transformation of Child Sacrifice in Judaism and Christianity* (New Haven, Conn.: Yale University Press, 1993) 232; Segal, *Rebecca's Children,* 179–81; Mary C. Boys, *Has God Only One Blessing? Judaism as a Source of Christian Self-Understanding* (Mahwah, N.J.: Paulist Press, 2000).

Bibliography

Arnal, William E., and Michel Desjardins, eds. *Whose Historical Jesus?* Studies in Christianity and Judaism 7. Waterloo, Ontario: Wilfrid Laurier Press, 1997.

Baird, J. Arthur. *The Justice of God in the Teaching of Jesus.* London: SCM Press, 1963.

Banks, Robert. *Jesus and the Law in the Synoptic Tradition.* Cambridge: Cambridge University Press, 1975.

Berkovits, E. "The Biblical Meaning of Justice." *Judaism* 18 (1969) 188–209.

Borg, Marcus J. *Jesus, a New Vision: Spirit, Culture, and the Life of Discipleship.* San Francisco: HarperCollins, 1987.

Boys, Mary C. *Has God Only One Blessing? Judaism as a Source of Christian Self-Understanding.* Mahwah, N.J.: Paulist Press, 2000.

Brown, Raymond E. *The Gospel According to John.* 2 vols. New York: Doubleday, 1966, 1970.

_____. "Not Jewish Christianity and Gentile Christianity, but Types of Jewish/Gentile Christianity." *Catholic Biblical Quarterly* 45 (1983) 74–9.

Brown, Raymond E., and John P. Meier. *Antioch and Rome: New Testament Cradles of Catholic Christianity.* Mahwah, N.J.: Paulist Press, 1983.

Brueggemann, Walter. *The Prophetic Imagination.* Philadelphia: Fortress Press, 1978.

Buber, Martin. *Moses: The Revelation and the Covenant.* New York: Harper & Row, 1958 (orig. 1946).

_____. *Two Types of Faith: A Study of the Interpenetration of Judaism and Christianity.* Trans. Norman P. Goldhawk. New York: Harper & Row, 1961 (orig. 1951).

Carroll, James. *Constantine's Sword: The Church and the Jews: A History.* Boston: Houghton Mifflin, 2001.

Carter, Warren. *What Are They Saying About Matthew's Sermon on the Mount?* Mahwah, N.J.: Paulist Press, 1994.

Charlesworth, James H., ed. *Jesus' Jewishness: Exploring the Place of Jesus within Early Judaism.* New York: Crossroad, 1991.

_____, ed. *Jesus and the Dead Sea Scrolls.* New York: Doubleday, 1992.

Charlesworth, James H., and Loren L. Johns, eds. *Hillel and Jesus: Comparisons of Two Major Religious Leaders.* Minneapolis: Fortress Press, 1997.

Clifford, Richard J. *Fair Spoken and Persuading: An Interpretation of Second Isaiah.* New York: Paulist Press, 1984.

Cohn-Sherbok, Dan. *Rabbinic Perspectives on the New Testament.* Lewiston, N.Y.: Edwin Mellen Press, 1990.

Cook, Michael L. *Christology as Narrative Quest.* Collegeville: The Liturgical Press, 1997.

_____. "Faith." *The HarperCollins Encyclopedia of Catholicism.* Ed. Richard P. McBrien. New York: Harper SanFrancisco, 1995.

_____. *The Historical Jesus.* Chicago: Thomas More Press, 1986.

_____. "Jesus from the Other Side of History: Christology in Latin America." *Theological Studies* 44 (June 1983) 258–87.

_____. *The Jesus of Faith: A Study in Christology.* Mahwah, N.J.: Paulist Press, 1981.

_____. "Jesus' Parables and the Faith That Does Justice." *Studies in the Spirituality of Jesuits* 24:5 (November 1992) 1–35.

Coote, Robert B. "Hapiru, Apiru." *Eerdmans Dictionary of the Bible.* Ed. David Noel Freedman. Grand Rapids, Mich.: Eerdmans Publishing, 2000.

Cross, Frank Moore. *Canaanite Myth and Hebrew Epic.* Cambridge, Mass.: Harvard University Press, 1973.

_____. *From Epic to Canon: History and Literature in Ancient Israel.* Baltimore: Johns Hopkins University Press, 1998.

Crossan, John Dominic. *The Historical Jesus: The Life of a Mediterranean Jewish Peasant.* San Francisco: HarperCollins, 1991.

Davies, Alan, ed. *Anti-Semitism and the Foundations of Christianity.* Mahwah, N.J.: Paulist Press, 1979.

Donahue, John R. "Biblical Perspectives on Justice." *The Faith That Does Justice: Examining the Christian Sources for Social Change.* Ed. John C. Haughey. New York: Paulist Press, 1977.

_____. *What Does the Lord Require? A Bibliographical Essay on the Bible and Social Justice.* Rev. and expanded. St. Louis: Institute of Jesuit Sources, 2000.

Dunn, James D. G., ed. *Jews and Christians: The Parting of the Ways: A.D. 70 to 135.* Grand Rapids, Mich.: Eerdmans Publishing, 1999 (orig. 1992).

Dunne, John S. *The Way of All the Earth.* New York: Macmillan, 1972.

Fisher, Eugene J., ed. *Visions of the Other: Jewish and Christian Theologians Assess the Dialogue.* Mahwah, N.J.: Paulist Press, 1994.

Flannery, Edward H. *The Anguish of the Jews: Twenty-Three Centuries of Antisemitism.* Rev. and updated. Mahwah, N.J.: Paulist Press, 1985.

Freedman, David Noel, ed. "Righteousness." *The Anchor Bible Dictionary.* Vol. 5. New York: Doubleday, 1992.

Fretheim, Terence E., and Karlfried Froehlich. *The Bible as Word of God in a Post-Modern Age.* Minneapolis: Fortress Press, 1998.

Freyne, Sean. *Galilee, Jesus and the Gospels.* Philadelphia: Fortress Press, 1988.

Frymer-Kensky, Tikva, and others, eds. *Christianity in Jewish Terms.* Boulder, Colo.: Westview Press, 2000.

Girard, René. *I See Satan Fall Like Lightning.* Trans. James G. Williams. Maryknoll, N.Y.: Orbis Books, 2001 (orig. 1999).

Hanson, Paul D. *The People Called: The Growth of Community in the Bible.* San Francisco: Harper & Row, 1986.

Harrington, Daniel J. *God's People in Christ: New Testament Perspectives on the Church and Judaism.* Philadelphia: Fortress Press, 1980.

Hartin, Patrick J. *A Spirituality of Perfection: Faith in Action in the Letter of James.* Collegeville: The Liturgical Press, 1999.

Harvey, Van A. *The Historian and the Believer: A Confrontation Between the Modern Historian's Principles of Judgment and the Christian's Will-to-Believe.* Philadelphia: Westminster Press, 1984 (orig. 1966).

Hassan, Riffat. "Messianism and Islam." *Journal of Ecumenical Studies* 22 (Spring 1985) 261–91.

Hengel, Martin. *The Charismatic Leader and His Followers.* Trans. James Greig. New York: Crossroad, 1981.

Herzog, Frederick. *God-Walk: Liberation Shaping Dogmatics.* Maryknoll, N.Y.: Orbis Books, 1988.

_____. *Justice Church: The New Function of the Church in North American Christianity.* Maryknoll, N.Y.: Orbis Books, 1980.

Herzog, William R. *Jesus, Justice, and the Reign of God: A Ministry of Liberation.* Louisville: Westminster John Knox Press, 2000.

_____. *Parables as Subversive Speech: Jesus as Pedagogue of the Oppressed.* Louisville: Westminster John Knox Press, 1994.

Heschel, Abraham J. *The Prophets.* 2 vols. Peabody, Mass.: Prince Press, 1962 (reprint HarperCollins, 1969, 1999).

Ho, Ahuva. *Sedeq and Sedaqah in the Hebrew Bible.* New York: Peter Lang, 1991.

Holmgren, Frederick C. *The Old Testament and the Significance of Jesus: Embracing Change—Maintaining Christian Identity.* Grand Rapids, Mich.: Eerdmans Publishing, 1999.

Holtz, Barry W., ed. *Back to the Sources: Reading the Classic Jewish Texts.* New York: Simon and Schuster, 1984.

Horsley, Richard A. *Sociology and the Jesus Movement.* New York: Crossroad, 1989.

Isaac, Jules. *The Teaching of Contempt: Christian Roots of Anti-Semitism.* Trans. Helen Weaver. Biographical intro. Claire Huchet Bishop. New York: Holt, Rinehart and Winston, 1964.

James, William. *The Varieties of Religious Experience.* New York: Collier, 1961.

Janzen, Waldemar. *Old Testament Ethics: A Paradigmatic Approach.* Louisville: Westminster John Knox Press, 1994.

Jeremias, Joachim. *New Testament Theology: The Proclamation of Jesus.* New York: Scribner's, 1971.

Johnson, Luke T. "The New Testament's Anti-Jewish Slander and the Conventions of Ancient Polemic." *Journal of Biblical Literature* 108 (1989) 419–41.

Kaesemann, Ernst. *Essays on New Testament Themes.* London: SCM Press, 1964.

Klenicki, Leon, and Geoffrey Wigoder, eds. *A Dictionary of the Jewish Christian Dialogue.* Expanded edition. Mahwah, N.J.: Paulist Press, 1995.

Lapide, Pinchas, and Ulrich Luz. *Jesus in Two Perspectives: A Jewish-Christian Dialog.* Trans. Lawrence W. Denef. Minneapolis: Augsburg, 1985.

Lee, Bernard J. *The Galilean Jewishness of Jesus: Retrieving the Jewish Origins of Christianity.* Mahwah, N.J.: Paulist Press, 1988.

_____. *Jesus and the Metaphors of God: The Christs of the New Testament.* Mahwah, N.J.: Paulist Press, 1993.

Levenson, Jon D. *The Death and Resurrection of the Beloved Son: The Transformation of Child Sacrifice in Judaism and Christianity.* New Haven, Conn.: Yale University Press, 1993.

_____. *The Hebrew Bible, the Old Testament, and Historical Criticism.* Louisville: Westminster John Knox Press, 1993.

_____. "Is There a Counterpart in the Hebrew Bible to New Testament Antisemitism?" *Journal of Ecumenical Studies* 22 (Spring 1985) 242–60.

_____. *Sinai and Zion: An Entry into the Jewish Bible.* Minneapolis: Winston Press, 1985; San Francisco: Harper & Row, 1987.

Lohfink, Norbert. *The Covenant Never Revoked: Biblical Reflections on Christian-Jewish Dialogue.* Trans. John J. Scullion. Mahwah, N.J.: Paulist Press, 1991.

_____. *Option for the Poor: The Basic Principle of Liberation Theology in the Light of the Bible.* Trans. Linda M. Maloney. N. Richland Hills, Tex.: BIBAL Press, 1995 (1987).

_____. *Theology of the Pentateuch: Themes of the Priestly Narrative and Deuteronomy.* Trans. Linda M. Maloney. Minneapolis: Fortress Press, 1994.

Lohfink, Norbert, and Erich Zenger. *The God of Israel and the Nations: Studies in Isaiah and the Psalms.* Trans. Everett R. Kalin. Collegeville: The Liturgical Press, 2000.

Malchow, Bruce V. *Social Justice in the Hebrew Bible.* Collegeville: The Liturgical Press, 1996.

Malina, Bruce J. *The New Testament World: Insights from Cultural Anthropology.* 3d ed., rev. and expanded. Louisville: Westminster John Knox Press, 2001.

_____. *The Social Gospel of Jesus: The Kingdom of God in Mediterranean Perspective.* Minneapolis: Fortress Press, 2001.

McDermott, John J. *What Are They Saying About the Formation of Israel?* Mahwah, N.J.: Paulist Press, 1998.

McKnight, Scot. *A New Vision for Israel: The Teachings of Jesus in National Context.* Grand Rapids, Mich.: Eerdmans Publishing, 1999.

Meier, John P. "Are There Historical Links between the Historical Jesus and the Christian Ministry?" *Theology Digest* 47 (2000) 303–15.

_____. "The Eucharist at the Last Supper: Did It Happen?" *Theology Digest* 42 (1995) 335–51.

_____. *A Marginal Jew: Rethinking the Historical Jesus.* 3 vols. New York: Doubleday, 1991, 1994, 2001.

Meyer, Ben F. *The Aims of Jesus.* London: SCM Press, 1979.

_____. *Christus Faber: The Master-Builder and the House of God.* Allison Park, Pa.: Pickwick Publications, 1992.

_____. *The Early Christians: Their World Mission and Self-Discovery.* Wilmington, Del.: Michael Glazier, 1986.

_____. "The Initial Self-Understanding of the Church." *Catholic Biblical Quarterly* XXVII (1965) 35–42.

_____. "Jesus and the Remnant of Israel." *Journal of Biblical Literature* LXXXIV (1965) 123–30.

Murphy, Séamus. "The Many Ways of Justice." *Studies in the Spirituality of Jesuits* 26:2 (March 1994) 1–40.

Neusner, Jacob. *Jews and Christians: The Myth of a Common Tradition.* London: SCM Press, 1991.

_____. *A Rabbi Talks with Jesus.* Rev. ed. Montreal; Ithaca, N.Y.: McGill-Queen's University Press, 2000.

_____. *Rabbinic Judaism: Structure and System.* Minneapolis: Fortress Press, 1995.

_____. *Telling Tales: Making Sense of Christian and Judaic Nonsense: The Urgency and Basis for Judeo-Christian Dialogue.* Louisville: Westminster John Knox Press, 1993.

_____. *The Theology of the Oral Torah: Revealing the Justice of God.* Montreal: McGill-Queen's University Press, 1999.

Newman, Carey C., ed. *Jesus and the Restoration of Israel: A Critical Assessment of N. T. Wright's Jesus and the Victory of God.* Downers Grove, Ill.: InterVarsity Press, 1999.

Nicholson, Ernest W. *God and His People: Covenant and Theology in the Old Testament.* Oxford: Clarendon Press, 1986.

Ochs, Peter, ed. *The Return to Scripture in Judaism and Christianity: Essays in Postcritical Scriptural Interpretation.* Mahwah, N.J.: Paulist Press, 1993.

Osiek, Carolyn. *What Are They Saying about the Social Setting of the New Testament?* Rev. and expanded. New York: Paulist Press, 1992.

Park, Andrew Sung, and Susan L. Nelson, eds. *The Other Side of Sin: Woundedness from the Perspective of the Sinned-Against.* Albany: State University of New York Press, 2001.

Pawlikowski, John T. *What Are They Saying about Christian-Jewish Relations?* New York: Paulist Press, 1980.

Pawlikowski, John T., and Hayim Goren Perelmuter, eds. *Reinterpreting Revelation and Tradition: Jews and Christians in Conversation.* Franklin, Wisc.: Sheed & Ward, 2000.

Pilch, John J. *Healing in the New Testament: Insights from Medical and Mediterranean Anthropology.* Minneapolis: Fortress Press, 2000.

Plaskow, Judith. *Standing Again at Sinai: Judaism from a Feminist Perspective.* San Francisco: Harper & Row, 1990.

Pleins, J. David. *The Psalms: Songs of Tragedy, Hope, and Justice.* Maryknoll, N.Y.: Orbis Books, 1993.

_____. *The Social Visions of the Hebrew Bible: A Theological Introduction.* Louisville: Westminster John Knox Press, 2001.

Ratzinger, Joseph. *Many Religions—One Covenant: Israel, the Church and the World.* Trans. Graham Harrison. San Francisco: Ignatius Press, 1999.

Reinhartz, Adele. *Befriending the Beloved Disciple: A Jewish Reading of the Gospel of John.* New York: Continuum, 2001.

Reiser, Marius. *Jesus and Judgment: The Eschatological Proclamation in Its Jewish Context.* Trans. Linda M. Maloney. Minneapolis: Fortress Press, 1997.

Reventlow, Henning Graf, and Yair Hoffman, eds. *Justice and Righteousness: Biblical Themes and Their Influence.* Sheffield: Sheffield Academic Press, 1992.

Richardson, Peter. *Herod, King of the Jews and Friend of Romans.* Columbia: University of South Carolina Press, 1996.

Riches, John. *Jesus and the Transformation of Judaism.* New York: Seabury Press, 1982.

Rieger, Joerg. *Remember the Poor: The Challenge to Theology in the Twenty-First Century.* Harrisburg, Pa.: Trinity Press International, 1998.

Ruether, Rosemary Radford. *Faith and Fratricide: The Theological Roots of Anti-Semitism.* New York: Seabury Press, 1974.

Sakenfeld, Katharine Doob. *Faithfulness in Action: Loyalty in Biblical Perspective.* Philadelphia: Fortress Press, 1985.

Saldarini, Anthony J. *Matthew's Christian-Jewish Community.* Chicago: University of Chicago Press, 1994.

_____. *Pharisees, Scribes and Sadducees in Palestinian Society.* Wilmington, Del.: Michael Glazier, 1988 (reprint: Grand Rapids, Mich.: Eerdmans Publishing; Livonia: Dove Booksellers, 2001, with a new foreword by James C. VanderKam).

Sanders, E. P. *Jesus and Judaism.* Philadelphia: Fortress Press, 1985.

_____. *Jewish Law from Jesus to the Mishnah.* London: SCM Press; Philadelphia: Trinity Press International, 1990.

_____. *Paul and Palestinian Judaism: A Comparison of Patterns of Religion.* Philadelphia: Fortress Press, 1977.

Sandmel, Samuel. *We Jews and Jesus.* New York: Oxford University Press, 1965.

Schearing, Linda S., and Steven L. McKenzie, eds. *Those Elusive Deuteronomists: The Phenomenon of Pan-Deuteronomism.* Sheffield: Sheffield Academic Press, 1999.

Schneiders, Sandra M. *The Revelatory Text: Interpreting the New Testament as Sacred Scripture.* 2d ed. Collegeville: The Liturgical Press, 1999.

_____. *Written That You May Believe: Encountering Jesus in the Fourth Gospel.* New York: Crossroad, 1999.

Schüssler Fiorenza, Elisabeth. *Bread Not Stone: The Challenge of Feminist Biblical Interpretation.* Boston: Beacon Press, 1984.

_____. *Rhetoric and Ethic: The Politics of Biblical Studies.* Minneapolis: Fortress Press, 1999.

Segal, Alan F. *Rebecca's Children: Judaism and Christianity in the Roman World.* Cambridge, Mass.: Harvard University Press, 1986.

Shanks, Hershel, ed. *Christianity and Rabbinic Judaism: A Parallel History of Their Origins and Early Development.* Washington, D.C.: Biblical Archaeology Society, 1992.

Shanks, Hershel, William G. Dever, Baruch Halpern, and P. Kyle McCarter Jr. *The Rise of Ancient Israel.* Washington, D.C.: Biblical Archaeology Society, 1992.

Smiga, George M. *Pain and Polemic: Anti-Judaism in the Gospels.* Mahwah, N.J.: Paulist Press, 1992.

Spiegel, Shalom. *The Last Trial.* Trans. Judah Goldin. Woodstock, Vt.: Jewish Lights Publishing, 1993 (orig. 1950).

Tan, Kim Huat. *The Zion Traditions and the Aims of Jesus.* Cambridge: Cambridge University Press, 1997.

Thoma, Clemens, and Michael Wyschogrod, eds. *Parable and Story in Judaism and Christianity.* Mahwah, N.J.: Paulist Press, 1989.

_____. *Understanding Scripture: Explorations of Jewish and Christian Traditions of Interpretation.* Mahwah, N.J.: Paulist Press, 1987.

Topel, L. John. *Children of a Compassionate God: A Theological Exegesis of Luke 6:20-49.* Collegeville: The Liturgical Press, 2001.

Tracy, David. "The Particularity and Universality of Christian Revelation." *Revelation and Experience.* Ed. Edward Schillebeeckx and Bas van Iersel, 106–16. New York: Seabury Press, 1979.

Veling, Terry A. *Living in the Margins: Intentional Communities and the Art of Interpretation.* New York: Crossroad, 1996.

Vermes, Geza. *Jesus and the World of Judaism.* Philadelphia: Fortress Press, 1983.

_____. *Jesus the Jew: A Historian's Reading of the Gospels.* London: Collins, 1973.

Walsh, J.P.M. *The Mighty from Their Thrones: Power in the Biblical Tradition.* Philadelphia: Fortress Press, 1987.

Weinfeld, Moshe. "The Covenant of Grant in the Old Testament and in the Ancient Near East." *Journal of the American Oriental Society* 90 (1970) 184–203.

_____. *Social Justice in Ancient Israel and in the Ancient Near East.* Jerusalem: Magnes Press; Minneapolis: Fortress Press, 1995.

Wiesel, Elie. *Messengers of God.* New York: Random House, 1976.

Williams, James G. *The Bible, Violence, and the Sacred: Liberation from the Myth of Sanctioned Violence.* Valley Forge, Pa.: Trinity Press International, 1991.

Wolters, Al. "The Text of the Old Testament." *The Face of Old Testament Studies: A Survey of Contemporary Approaches.* Ed. D. W. Baker and B. T. Arnold, 19–37. Grand Rapids, Mich.: Baker Books, 1999.

Worth, Roland H., Jr. *The Sermon on the Mount: Its Old Testament Roots.* Mahwah, N.J.: Paulist Press, 1997.

Wright, N. T. *Jesus and the Victory of God.* Minneapolis: Fortress Press, 1996.

Young, Brad H. *Jesus and His Jewish Parables: Rediscovering the Roots of Jesus' Teaching.* Mahwah, N.J.: Paulist Press, 1989.

_____. *Jesus the Jewish Theologian.* Peabody, Mass.: Hendrickson, 1995.

Index of Subjects